Rugby's Greatest |
Who really was F.S. Jackson?

Tom Mather

London League Publications Ltd

Rugby's Greatest Mystery
Who really was F.S. Jackson?

© Tom Mather. Foreword © Graham Morris. Appendix 2 © Graham Williams & Peter Lush
The moral right of Tom Mather to be identified as the author has been asserted.

Cover design © Stephen McCarthy.

Front cover: Photo of Jackson published by *The Sketcher* souvenir. No.. 25. Auckland, 25 July, 1908. p.11: Four British rugby players. (Courtesy Alexander Turnbull Library, Wellington, New Zealand) and F.S. Jackson in later life, photo Irwin Jackson. Back cover: The 1908 Anglo-Welsh Rugby Union team that toured New Zealand. Jackson is in the middle of the back row.

A CIP catalogue record for this book is available from the British Library.

This paperback edition first published in Great Britain in March 2012 by:
London League Publications Ltd, P.O. Box 65784, London NW2 9NS

ISBN: 978-1903659-60-1

Cover design by: Stephen McCarthy Graphic Design
                               46, Clarence Road, London N15 5BB

Layout: Peter Lush

Printed and bound in Great Britain by Charlesworth Press, Wakefield

Foreword

I have known Tom Mather for more years than probably he or I care to remember. During that time he has put together some of the most diverse and fascinating books imaginable on the subject of rugby league, be it the fictional diary (although based on fact) of a legendary Northern Union player, a study of rugby league under floodlights or a sad, but welcome tribute to some of the code's fallen heroes of two world wars. All of them represent unexplored territory as far as subjects for rugby league literature is concerned but Tom's latest effort unravelling the life of the player known as Frederick Stanley Jackson has, in my opinion, provided him with his biggest challenge of all.

As someone who conversed with Tom on a regular basis throughout his relentless search into the truth behind a man whose real identity was as elusive as that of the Scarlet Pimpernel, I have to confess I became more and more amazed each time he announced his latest revelation to me. Tom often used me, I think, as a sounding board as he sought to bounce a few ideas around that had surfaced since our last conversation. It was something I was delighted to do. When the phone rang, and on hearing Tom's familiar voice at the other end, I waited with bated breath to learn of the latest twist and turn in a story that, rather than emerging into the clear light of day, often became more bizarre and unexpected with each instalment.

Of course, much of what Tom uncovered did provide him with answers to nagging problems as he joined up a few more hitherto unresolved 'loose ends', but more, much more of what he discovered contradicted his earlier finds. It seemed in my mind – but obviously not in Tom's - to make the task of obtaining the real truth behind the man look improbable, nay impossible. To me it developed into a tale of mystery that was as intriguing as any case undertaken by Jackson's mythical contemporary Sherlock Holmes. Not so much a 'Who done it?' but more of a 'Who was it?' as each revelation became more remarkable than the previous.

I often get in touch with Tom to pick his brain for information or to ask some small favour. He will do likewise whenever the need arises and this was frequently the case during 2009 as he put together his excellent account of the first Northern Union tour to Australasia in 1910, a story that was long overdue its place on the rugby league bookshelf. As Tom explains in the pages that follow, it was during that pioneering tour that Fred Jackson, a former Northern Union and rugby union player from England, represented New Zealand against the British tourists. For Tom, it was simply not enough to mention that basic fact. Like all true historians he wanted to get a bit more background on the man and how it was that he ended up on a pitch in Auckland to face his countrymen that day. Of course, as I have already implied, the truth was not about to stare Tom in the face as he may have originally anticipated. Instead, he found himself travelling down a complicated and roughly laid out roadway. But one thing I have learnt over the years about my Fylde-based colleague is that he relishes exploring the unknown, as proved by the earlier publications referred to at the start of this piece.

What probably began in Tom's head as a paragraph in his story of that 1910 tour took on a life of its own. Jackson's amazing tale became one that demanded telling. Looking at the finished result of Tom's labours – labours that included not an inconsiderable amount of detective work (Hercule Poirot step aside!) – we are presented with an account of a man who appears to have done all in his power to keep his identity and early years private. Like all the best novels fate decreed that the new life and identity Jackson created for himself in the 'Land of the Silver Fern' some 100 years ago would eventually lead to revealing the truth behind his mystique. Jackson and his secrets were waiting to be discovered and I, for one, am glad it fell into Tom's lap as many a researcher – probably myself included – would have thrown in the towel after round one. I congratulate Tom on his achievement in bringing together a story that goes beyond the bounds of rugby as played on the field and tells a tale so incredible that you would not believe it unless, of course, it happened to be true.

Graham Morris

About the author

Tom Mather has, over the last few years, written a number of books about the game of rugby league in collaboration with London League Publications Ltd, along with books that were self-published. The books have included *Calm in the Cauldron* with John Dorahy, *The Best in the Northern Union*, detailing the events of the first ever tour 'down under' by the Lions in 1910 and *Snuff out the Moon* that covered the development of floodlit rugby, all with London League Publications Ltd. *Missing in Action* was a book that told of the lives of 13 players who were killed in either World War One or World War Two. He also co-wrote *The Iceman*, the autobiography of former Wigan coach John Monie, which was published by Mainstream Publishing

As a result of his work on *The Best in the Northern Union* the Rugby Football League produced a replica of the 1910 tour shirt which they wore when they played New Zealand in 2010 to celebrate the 100th anniversary of the first ever test between the two countries played in New Zealand.

This latest offering breaks new ground as it deals with a man of mystery who played both codes at the very highest level in two countries, but whose true identity remained unknown to the world until now.

Tom Mather is married and lives with his wife Janet in Lytham on the north west coast of England, and is the father of Barrie-Jon Mather, the former Wigan, Perth and Castleford rugby league player who is now the performance director for the RFL.

Introduction

This is a remarkable book for many reasons. First there is the manner in which it was conceived, as a result of a single comment made to me about a rugby player. Second, there is the fact that the story starts in the middle rather than the beginning, travels to the end and then back to the beginning. Third is the quite remarkable rugby player of both codes whose life this book attempts to describe. For most of his life he used an alias and was extremely secretive about his early life; even, it could be said, bordering on the obsessive. He cocked a snoot at the rugby authorities of two codes in two countries whom he felt had let him down, but still forged a career on the rugby fields of England and New Zealand in both union and league.

While it is a book about a sportsman, it is more than that. It is a detective story that attempts to uncover the truth behind the mystery, intrigue and deception that permeated the whole of his adult life. It also attempts to solve a mystery that has puzzled the rugby world for over 100 years.

Finally, there is the remarkable dynasty that he established in his adopted country, on-and-off the rugby field. His offspring not only excelled at rugby union gaining All-Black and Maori caps, but also went on to become activists for Maori rights and trade unionism for the Maori. That a Pakeha (non-Maori) could achieve so much for the Maori in New Zealand speaks volumes about the man whose life is contained in these pages. He was a man who would always stand at the shoulder of anyone who was suffering injustice or persecution even to the detriment of himself.

If that were not enough, there is the quite remarkable investigation that was undertaken in England, South Africa, Wales and New Zealand that would eventually lead to the revelation of his true identity over 100 years after he took great pains to hide it from the world. In doing so it enabled some of his family in New Zealand to finally know the true identity of the loving kindly man they knew as their grandfather, although it has to be said that they do not accept the results of my research. In Great Britain it allowed his other family to know at long last just what happened to the 'black sheep' of the family.

Tom Mather
January 2012

Acknowledgements

There are a great many people to thank who contributed so much to the detective work needed to produce this book. In Australia: Sean Fagan the rugby league historian and owner of *RL1908.com* website for all his help and encouragement and for kick-starting the project in the first place. In New Zealand: Don Hammond from the New Zealand Rugby League museum, John Coffey - the rugby league reporter, Bernie Wood - the rugby league historian and Moana Jackson the grandson of Fred Jackson. Many of the newspaper quotes used and photographs are courtesy of the New Zealand National Library and their excellent Paperspast web site.

In the United Kingdom, Kim Cooper of the Cornwall Reference Library Centre, Katrina Coopey of the Cardiff Reference Library and Howard Evans, the Welsh rugby union historian and journalist, for help with the Welsh side of the story; John Edwards, who is a font of all knowledge on Swinton Rugby League club; the library staff at the Rugby Union Museum in Twickenham for the minutes of committee meetings and other information from 1908. Many thanks to Glyn Gabe and Val Gabe. Glyn, aged 93, was a valuable source of information.

There are three other people who deserve a special mention for their efforts in seeing this book into publication. The first is Graham Morris who acted as a springboard for my many theories and for the unstinting aid and guidance he gave along with many new possible avenues of research. Second, Yvonne Chisholm, who was fantastic in the amount of new material she unearthed and verified about Jackson, much of it unseen for over 100 years. Her genealogy skills coupled with a love of both rugby and a mystery enabled the final enigma of just who Jackson really was to be solved. To her go my eternal thanks for the unselfish manner in which she has shared information with me that she had discovered about Jackson. Finally to my wife Janet for the technical and word processing skills that have proved to be invaluable in the production of this manuscript and the photographs included in the book. If I have forgotten anyone please excuse my ignorance and put it down to my increased age and onrushing senility.

I would also like to thank my publishers, Peter Lush and Dave Farrar, Graham Williams for his work on the Appendix on Leicester Tigers, Huw Richards who read the draft, and everyone else who contributed to the production of the book, including Steve McCarthy who designed the cover and the staff of Charlesworth Press who printed it.

Tom Mather
January 2012

Contents

1. Who is Jackson?

In 1908 the game of rugby union and its leadership faced a monumental scandal that threatened to cause even more problems only 13 years after the great split of 1895. It was a scandal that would envelop not only the leadership of the Rugby Football Union (RFU) but also the rugby union Anglo-Welsh tourists in New Zealand. Once again the problem was one of professionalism within the amateur game. There was a belief that certain clubs and parts of the country were turning a blind eye to covert payments to players while others were rooting it out with almost religious like zeal.

Rugby union had been decimated in the industrial north by the formation of the Northern Union (NU), which would become rugby league, in 1895. A murky compromise between the RFU and the Welsh Football Union over the testimonial given to the famous Newport player Arthur Gould had prevented a further split in the game which could have left rugby union with its only major base in London and the South East of England. The Irish and Scottish Unions had refused to participate in the tour to Wales because they felt that the 1905 All Blacks had been professionals because they paid their players expenses of 3/- (15p) a day. This showed the huge tensions in the game over the 'professionalism' issue. Internationally, Northern Union rugby was starting to develop in Australia and New Zealand, and would soon overtake rugby union as the major winter football code in Australia.

The scandal threatened the very fabric of the game in the Midlands and involved the Leicester club in particular. Leicester, unlike most rugby union clubs, had developed along commercial lines and operated as an 'invitation' club, inviting members of other clubs to play, rather than as an open members club which was the norm for most clubs. Their recruitment policy had caused animosity from local rivals, and raised questions about how they fitted into the RFU's amateur ethos.

At the centre of the allegations of professionalism was one player, Frederick Stanley Jackson[*], who was at the top of his game.

However, the focus of this book is not whether Jackson was a professional player, as defined by the RFU. The question is: what was the true identity of the Anglo-Welsh tourist accused of professionalism and called home from that 1908 tour?

---

[*] Not to be confused with the well-known cricketer of the same name, although the choice of a famous sportsman as a pseudonym was not believed to be coincidental.

It seems that he had at least three aliases which were raised as the scandal began to dominate the sports pages of the newspapers. That question has never been satisfactorily answered until now.

The allegations and counter-allegations about him were a major part of the disputes which threatened to tear rugby union apart. This is the story of that troubled time and the effects it had on the player himself. From a wider point of view, the stakes were very high. Leicester was the dominant club in midlands rugby. Had they been driven out of rugby union for professionalism, their only alternative home would have been the Northern Union, because any rugby union team playing against them would have been deemed to have 'professionalised' themselves. Today, with union and league teams sharing grounds, players and even club names, it is easy to forget how deep and bitter the split between the two codes was only 13 years after the 1895 split.

In every era and in every sport there are sportsmen who come to the fore. They capture the sporting public's imagination. At the beginning of the 20th century, with cinema in its infancy, the newspapers were the only means people had to find out about sportsmen and their exploits. It was the sports reporter and what they wrote that conveyed to the general public the prowess of the players. The press then, as now, had the power to build up or bring down any sporting figure and used it constantly.

One such sportsman who both benefited and suffered at the hands of the local, national and international press was the player we shall refer to as Fred Jackson. His full name, or rather the name he was known by for the longest period of his life, was Frederick Stanley Jackson. He was a rugby union player who played for Leicester. He joined the club in the 1905–06 season as a powerful, strong, running forward who was also capable of booting a football prodigious distances with great accuracy. He was a try scorer and a very good goalkicker, in other words he was every sports journalist's dream.

Jackson very quickly came to the attention of the Leicester sports writers. He also quickly won over the Leicester supporters with his displays on the field. Such were his performances that after a short time whenever he donned the Leicester shirt the national sports correspondents became aware of this West Country boy whose previous claims to fame had been as a member of the Cornwall county team. He was a character that one could not miss on or off the field not only because he was for his time a giant of a man.

He was around five feet 11 inches tall and weighed 14 stones and seven pounds. His massive frame was topped by a shock of black hair that made him easily recognisable. There can be little doubt that in Leicester at that time he would have been thought of in the same light as Dean Richards was in his playing days. He was an all-action player who kicked goals with monotonous regularity and scored tries as well. It was the press attention that was ultimately to lead to his downfall.

But Fred Jackson's story is not straightforward. It is about a man and his early life, which was steeped not only in both rugby union and rugby league, but also for over 100 years shrouded in mystery. Everything known up to now about the early life of this man was whatever sports journalists of the day wrote about him and his exploits or what he wanted people to know and was prepared to reveal. He was secretive about his early life and at times cleverly manipulated facts about himself to suit his own ends. He did it so well that neither we nor his own family had any idea of his true identity, until now.

It is not clear how he made a living or supported himself in those far off days, although he may have had casual work, and was clearly physically fit. We have no idea either how he was able to fund his rugby career. At the time he was playing it was on the surface a game for the wealthy in many areas. There was an attitude among the game's leadership, particularly following the 'great schism' of 1895, that if you could not afford to play the game you should not play it. Rugby union was officially a game for the purely amateur player, and this was true in practice in many clubs. In the south of the country it was often the domain of the sons of wealthy families.

Even after the 1895 split, there were still some clubs which had working class players, but these tended to be in the poorer parts of the country. In some areas, the Midlands and the South West in particular, there were strong suspicions that players were paid, but that this was well hidden from the game's authorities in London. It is against this backdrop that the life of Fred Jackson is set.

In order to make sense of his story it is clearer to use the alias he used for the majority of his life, Frederick Stanley Jackson. To do otherwise would simply cause more confusion. At the outset it must be stressed this was not his true identity, for there is no record of him as Frederick Stanley Jackson in the 1891 or 1881 census records in the county of Cornwall where he often claimed that he was born. Piecing together details of his early life proved to be very difficult, for Jackson never spoke of events in his life prior to 1908 publicly to anyone, not even his own children.

Jackson claimed in early 1908, when he gained selection for the Anglo-Welsh team that was to tour New Zealand and Australia, that he had been born a Cornishman, first seeing the light of day in Camborne. Unfortunately, he did not reveal the date of his birth, but the available evidence suggests that his date of birth was sometime in 1878 or 1877.

This time frame is based on information he gave in an interview to a reporter for a Manchester evening paper in 1901. However, this was at the time when he had just joined the Northern Union side Swinton, using the name John R. Jones. Realising that playing for a NU semi-professional team would see him permanently banned from rugby union; he may – for once – have had good reason to be vague about his background. This date does seem to fit in quite well with what is known of his early life. It would also allow him to have done what he claims to have done.

The starting point for this information about Jackson was in a newspaper article, not in the United Kingdom, but in New Zealand. The *Taranaki Herald* on 26 May 1908 published an article which included pen pictures of the Anglo-Welsh tourists who had recently arrived in the country. The reporter claimed that because the details on the players had been supplied by the tour captain, Arthur 'Boxer'. Harding, they could safely be assumed to be correct. It seems obvious to suggest that Harding would have asked or been asked by a reporter for each player in the party to produce a short description of their career for release to the press. This is what was written about Jackson: "Born Camborne, educated at Camborne Mining School, and played in school football team, 1892–95, also cricket team same years. Played for Plymouth 1896–98, Leicester 1898–1908, Cornwall 1900–1908, and was captain in 1903–04."

Short, sharp and to the point and the information about his early life, which could not be verified by team-mates or reporters, is very misleading. It is now clear that he was not born in Cornwall, at least according to the census records. Further investigation showed that he originated in South Wales.

As regards his education; the Camborne Mining School was at this time one of the leading hard rock mining education establishments in the country. It took in students from top grammar schools up and down the country. Students would have to be aged at least 16 or over and have been educated to a high standard to qualify for a place at the school. If what Jackson claimed was true then he would have been at least 16 in 1892, and 32 when selected for the 1908 tour. This is feasible, but then his birth date would be 1876, rather than the 1878 or 1877 he claimed.

There is also the question of his education before going to the mining college. To have been admitted to the Camborne School of Mines he would have needed a good education, yet there is no record of this.

Another discrepancy is the claim he played for the school football team. The school shows no record of an F.S Jackson playing either cricket or rugby football at that time. There was an H.E Jackson; was this the same person? Jackson was quite good at throwing people off his trail by adopting aliases of famous sportsmen. There was an F.S. Jackson, who became in later life the Right Honourable Sir Frank Stanley Jackson, who played cricket for Yorkshire from 1890 to 1907, and captained England in 1905. It could well be that Fred simply took his name and used it as his own. Why he chose the name F.S. Jackson has never been explained.

There is no record of a Frederick Stanley Jackson attending Camborne Mining School around the period he claimed to be there. However, given the school's standing within the mining industry both here and abroad at the time, it was not uncommon for people to claim to have attended the school in the hope that it would assist them in the mining industry. Jackson later in life claimed to be a mining engineer, but there is no record either in Great Britain or New Zealand of him being employed in this role. In later life he worked as a council clerk and a groundsman at times, something that would have been unlikely had he been a qualified mining engineer.

Often when he played for Cornwall there were players from the Camborne School of Mines in the team. When the county won the championship for the first time in 1908, there were two other members of the pack, J.G. Milton and A.J. Wilson who played for, and attended, the mining college. He could have gleaned information about the school from them and others of similar ilk, enough to pass himself off as a past student of the school. In fact, as established through further investigation, his education and early training were far more humble.

However, his ability to play rugby union was unquestionable. In the pen picture he claims to have played for Plymouth and Cornwall. Both claims are true, and just before going on tour he was in the Cornwall side that won the County Championship in 1908. However, for some reason he fails to mention that he also played for Camborne before moving to Plymouth. Given this was supposedly his first club it seems curious that he would not put that into his 'pen-picture'. However, the

5

reason could be that he seems to have left Camborne to join Plymouth under somewhat acrimonious circumstances. There was an inference that he was induced to switch clubs for a monetary consideration. He also failed to mention that he also played for London Welsh and there were also claims that he turned out for Swansea. However, club affiliations were less fixed than today, and it was not unusual for players from one club to turn out as guests for another, or to join another club on a tour. He also claimed to have captained the Cornwall County side in 1903–04, but records clearly show he did not. It is surprising that Jackson claimed this in his pen picture, as other members of the party could have played against that Cornwall team.

In the second half of the 1890s, another famous young player was also playing for London Welsh outfit, a centre by the name of Rhys Gabe. It will become clear that later there was a family connection between the two of them. Gabe was attending Borough Road College at that time, training to become a teacher. Rhys Gabe went all through his life under that name although his given name was actually "Gape." Later on, when Jackson's identity was challenged, people claimed that he was 'Gabe' who had played in Swansea.

This was a period in his life when he was around the age of 18 to 20. The Victorian age was coming to its close and rugby, as was said, in the south was played mainly by the sons of the wealthy. If Jackson really was the son of a working class Cornishman, then it is highly likely that he would be working in the mines or on the land. The latter is more likely because in the 1880s the mining industry in Cornwall declined and many miners emigrated to South America or South Africa where their skills were still in demand. He would not be in a position to travel to Plymouth or to London to play rugby if he were working as a low paid worker on the land unless his travel and expenses were paid by the clubs. And if he was Cornish, why did he play for London Welsh?

Possibly he was not from a working class background, but rather from middle-class or a wealthy family. The other explanation could be that he was paid to play his rugby, or at least given generous expenses. There is also a more simple explanation, and that was that he was misleading about his background. There is evidence that indicates that he was well educated, certainly better than the average working class boy who would have left school by the age of 11 or 12 in those days. What he did next would support the latter suggestion.

Another common theme in what was known about Jackson at the time of the 1908 tour was that he had been in South Africa, possibly in the army, around the time of the Boer War, from 1899 to 1902.

He played both football codes, rugby union and association. In the latter he quickly gained a good reputation as a goalkeeper. It was reported that he was probably one of the top goalkeepers in the country. In rugby he quickly gained a reputation as a forward who was uncompromising both in attack and in defence. More importantly, given the high altitude in the Transvaal, his kicking ability, which was formidable at sea level, must have seemed prodigious at altitude, particularly with the heavy leather balls of the time.

In that same year the British Lions rugby union tourists landed in South Africa to take on the might of South Africa. The tourists landed in late June on a 21 match tour of the country. They were only defeated once, in the fourth test. Earlier research suggested that Jackson played against the tourists, but the British and Irish Lions match centre web site has no record of a Fred Jackson playing against the tourists. That said, while a Fred Jackson did not play, there is no way of knowing if he used another name while playing rugby in South Africa.

However, further research, outlined in chapter 14, established that in the 17th Duke of Cambridge's Own Lancers regiment that served in South Africa in 1900 there was only one Jackson and an F. Jackson at that. According to the medal roll F. Jackson was entitled to the Queen's Medal with three clasps. It would appear that these clasps were awarded for particular battles and the three that Jackson was awarded were 'Belfast', Cape Colony', and 'Orange Free State'. The latter two were relatively unimportant for the investigation because they referred to anyone who had seen any action throughout the entire conflict and were quite general in scope. However, the 'Belfast' clasp was much more important as it referred to a specific engagement that occurred between 26 and 27 August 1900.

This established that F. Jackson was in South Africa in 1900 and saw action. The regiment arrived there in February 1900. Most of the major battles were over and the army was mainly engaged in a cleaning up operation, but nonetheless Jackson saw action. So was the F. Jackson, regimental number 4266, really our Frederick Stanley Jackson? Sadly, there is no way of proving that one way or the other as his service records probably no longer exist. However, given these facts it is reasonable to assume that he was the F. Jackson on the medal roll. His record with the Legion of Frontiersmen and the Home Guard in the Second World War, along with his attempts to enlist and subsequent call up in the First World War make it likely that he was in South Africa. Also, throughout his life he always claimed to be a Boer War veteran.

If, as the evidence suggests, Jackson did enlist with the Lancers this would explain many of the anomalies about his early travels and time in South Africa. It would explain how at such a young age he was able to travel there from England and then cross the country. It would also explain how he was able to indulge his passion for sport. It also explains why research failed to throw up any evidence of Jackson working in the Transvaal, as he was in the army.

The only issue which is not answered is how he could join Swinton in 1901 while the war was still going on. Perhaps he had served the period he had signed up for, probably eight years, so was entitled to be discharged and shipped back to England. If he had signed on that period, as was usual then and was in York prior to 1898 in the middle years of his service, then by 1900 he would have served his time and be entitled to be released and return to England. This is supported by the Lancers regimental archivist who said that the Boer War was not 'a conscripted offensive' and once a soldier's term was completed then the army could not legally keep him and had to return him home.

But why did he always say that he had enlisted in a Transvaal regiment? He said he enlisted as a private and gained a commission, why? It meant that his claims could not be disproved. The records for these regiments were not as comprehensive as English ones, which are often not complete. Had he said he was in the Lancers that could have been checked and his true identity exposed, although that accepts that he used F. Jackson in the army. He said nothing of his military service while in New Zealand with the Anglo-Welsh tourists, presumably because some of his colleagues had served in the Boer War. Curiously, the cricketer F.S. Jackson also served in the army during the Boer War.

2. Northern Union with Swinton

Jackson left South Africa and returned to England from Gordon's Bay near Cape Town some time in 1900 or 1901. On his return it is alleged he travelled to Wales and began playing for the Swansea club. It is now that he uses another alias for the first time. He allegedly took the field for the Welsh club under the name of Ivor Gabe. However, according to the club history and club historian, there is no record of an Ivor Gabe turning out for the Swansea club around this time.

Once more it could well be that he never did play for Swansea or if he did he used another alias. What photographic records remain of that period in the club's history and there are a good number, fail to show Jackson or anyone even remotely resembling him. However, that is no reason to doubt that he played because he was notoriously shy of ever being photographed. Also, there is no record of a 'Gabe' playing for Swansea's near neighbours Llanelli or Neath around this time either. Nor is there any photographic evidence of players from those two clubs who resembled Jackson.

What is not in doubt is that by September 1901 Fred Jackson, or as he may well now have been calling himself, Ivor Gabe, had travelled up to Manchester and approached the Swinton Northern Union club with a view to signing for them as a professional player. Such a move does prompt the question: why Swinton? There were any number of clubs he could have approached if he wished to be paid for playing the game, so something must have drawn him to Manchester.

During his time in South Africa Jackson could well have come in contact with a player by the name of Gartrill who had a brother who played for Swinton around this time. It may well have been that he recommended that because Jackson was returning home he may like to try his luck with Swinton and his brother would put a good word in for him. Sadly the board meeting minutes of the Swinton club are very brief at this period in their history and show nothing about him signing.

However, when Jackson signed for Swinton he told them that his name was John R. Jones. It may well have been that he took that name simply because they were quite a number of players at the club called Jones when he arrived. One forward in particular was a G.R. Jones who had played for the club in a Challenge Cup Final. Jackson could have thought that J and G could easily be mistaken for each other. By adopting the same surname it would make it difficult for anyone to prove which Jones − if any − was actually Jackson or even Gabe. Once again he was taking steps to cover any trace of his identity from prying eyes. In addition, he was trying to ensure that the rugby union officials would not find out about his professional exploits.

If the Swinton playing records for the 1901–02 season are correct and Jackson really was the J.R. Jones that played for the club in the forwards then he really did play as a professional. During that season the records show there were only three players called Jones who played in the first team: a wingman G.H. Jones and forwards G. R. Jones and J.R. Jones. J. R. Jones made his debut against Hunslet on 28 September 1901, having first played for the 'A' team two weeks earlier against Stockport and the previous week against Birkenhead 'A'. His last appearance for the club came in a Challenge Cup quarter-final defeat to Broughton Rangers on 5 April 1902, a match in which he was injured. In total during the season he made 13 appearances for Swinton before disappearing from the scene. However, the records are not as accurate as first thought for G.R (Dick) Jones played a number of times during that season, with his appearances being credited to John (J.R.) Jones.

Swinton had been told by Jackson that he had been playing for Swansea and had just returned from South Africa. They made the assumption, as they would, that the Jones they had signed was a Welshman. Jackson did not disillusion them. Quite the contrary, he set about embellishing his new persona. As with all new signings for the club, the local press took an interest in John R. Jones the new Welsh signing and in September 1901 Jackson was interviewed by a reporter for the local press. In the interview he claimed to be 22 years old. If this were true then it would establish his year of birth as being either 1878 or 1879.

In that interview he also built up the new persona he had adopted for Swinton. He claimed to be a Welshman born in Morriston, then a village close to Swansea, and that he had been educated at Llandovery College back in Wales. The reporter had no reason to doubt the information Jackson had given him and did not seek confirmation of it. Had he done so he would have quickly discovered that Llandovery College had no record of a Jones matching Jackson's description. They had no record of a Jackson or a Gabe attending either for that matter.

The other thing is that nowhere in the interview is there any mention of Jones's, or should that be Gabe's, occupation or what he did off the field. It is this area which would have caused Jackson some worries. At that time in the Northern Union they were particularly vigilant with regard to players actually being in employment. This was due to the fact that they wanted people outside the game to see that professionalism was not the 'norm' within the Northern Union. To this end the rules stated that if a player had not worked in the week leading up to the game the ne was not allowed to play. This was so players could not be seen to be making a living solely from the game.

Jackson made his debut for Swinton on 28 September 1901 against Hunslet. The *Reporter* on 5 October said that Swinton had been granted a permit registration for Jones (i.e. Jackson). This suggested that he had missed a day or two from work through injury or some other reason. Whatever that reason was he needed to obtain permission to play due to time off from his place of work. This could have caused him a dilemma. He was playing for the club under an assumed name, Jones, but what name was he using in the work place, was he Jackson, Gabe or Jones? However, as Swinton is not a huge place, and players for the local rugby club would have been well-known in the town, if he was working in that area he probably used the name Jones. However, the report is one of the few indications found that suggests he was employed whilst he was playing his rugby.

Jackson meanwhile was doing his talking on the field albeit for a brief time only. It is interesting to note that when Swinton registered him as a player the RFL recorded him as being from 'Gordon's Cape Town' adding weight to the belief that he actually had been in South Africa. The also registered him under the name of J.R. Jones so they must have believed or been lead to believe that was his true identity.

The following article was published in the local Salford paper in 1901 while he was playing for Swinton. It is one of the rare occasions that Jackson spoke to the press and that interview was published. As can be seen it was a masterpiece of understatement.

The newspaper report said: "As an item out of the ordinary course of things, one of the playing members of the club has all through the season been surrounded by a sort of mystery which has given rise to all sorts of rumours as to his identity. We refer to the stalwart forward who is known to friends and opponents as 'Jack' Jones. It is an open secret that 'Jones' is only a name assumed for the period during which he plays football. As to his real identity – well Mr 'Jones' chooses for reasons best known to himself, to keep a strict secret. During the past week we have been fortunate enough to have a long conversation with the mysterious one, and have found him willing to converse on any subject only himself, which was, of course, our object in approaching the unknown.

For the benefit of Swintonians in particular we may say the 'Jones' is a Welshman, his football career commencing when he joined a team connected with Llandovery College, at which place our subject received his education. After leaving the college he went to London and for a couple of seasons was the most prominent forward in the London Welsh team. He assisted this club against Blackheath, Oxford and Cambridge Universities and all the other prominent rugby union organisations. In 1895 he left England to take up residence in the Transvaal, where he resided until the war broke out, and all business being practically suspended. 'Jones' joined one of the regiments then formed, and had about 18 months of the hardest fighting. We ought, however to mention that previous to hostilities commencing Jones played against the English teams who visited South Africa at both 'Socker' and 'Rugger' and in the first named code was reckoned the best goal-keeper in South Africa.

During last summer he returned to England and offered his services to Swinton, terms were arranged, and for the first time in his athletic career he turned out as a fully-fledged professional. Standing 5ft 10½ inches 'Jones' is of exceptionally fine physique and is one of the heaviest forwards in the Swinton team, as he scales no less than 14 stone 9 pounds. Though he has never scored any tangible points in the matches played, his work has always been useful and his efforts in the scrimmage have shown that he was no stranger to rugby football. Possessed of more than the average amount of education one instinctively feels after a few minutes' conversation that "Jones" has had a past which would be very interesting reading to everyone fond of adventure. His identity may leak out at some time or other, and it may cause something more than a mere flutter in local circles when it is found that we have been entertaining unawares for over six months one of the 'lions' of the athletic world."

Jackson did not play against the British Lions while in South Africa; well certainly not using the name Jackson. He may well have played against teams who had been in the country. Extensive research also shows that a Fred Jackson never attended Llandovery College around the time Jackson claims to have done so. There is also no record of a Jones from Morriston attending the college that fits Jackson's profile. The same holds true for a Gabe at the college.

Once again he is casting a web of deceit, but one that to the casual observer would seem very plausible. What the article does, however, is support the idea that Jackson did spend some time with London Welsh, for back then, as in modern times, the club recruited a good number of its players from old boys of Llandovery College. Hence the reporter said that Jackson had begun his rugby career with a club connected to that college. It could well have been that he learned about the Llandovery College by listening to the old boys talking at the London Welsh club.

It is odd also that the article seems to suggest it was an open secret at Swinton that Jones was not his real name, yet the club and the reporter were quite happy to let the situation continue as were the Northern Union. However, it was a situation that rugby union also turned a blind eye to as shall be seen later in his career. Northern Union clubs would often give trial matches to rugby union players and hide their identities to try to ensure they did not face suspension if they returned to that code. They would refer to them as A.N.Other or S.O.Else. However, in this case the Northern Union actually registered him as a Swinton player under the name of J.R. Jones when the local paper had said this was a pseudonym. It was not unknown for players to play under pseudonyms at this time for various reasons, and the NU seems to have accepted his registration without question.

The other interesting fact is the view formed by the reporter that Jones possessed more than the average amount of education. Once more this is evidence supporting the view that he had an education well above that for an average working class man. Where he gained this education was and still remains a mystery. Jones disappeared from the scene as quickly as he arrived and in equally mysterious circumstances. It was not the first time he disappeared in the short time he was with the club.

The minutes of the Swinton club at that time make no mention of how Jackson arrived at the club. Was he spotted by a club scout or did he simply turn up on the doorstep asking for a trial? The latter is more likely. The club must have been impressed by what they initially saw, impressed enough to pay him £40 to sign professional forms for the club. He made only 13 appearances for the club before moving on. Perhaps he was coming under pressure from the club or the Northern Union authorities to show he was in 'bona-fide' employment. If he was not or was working under another name, he would then have a problem. Or it could well be that the Northern Union had caught on to the fact that Jones was not his real name and were pushing him to state just who he really was.

Given the period in the history of the game, however, in my opinion perhaps the authorities took the view that it was better to let 'sleeping dogs lie'. What is not disputed is Jackson's habit of disappearing from the scene for a period of time. With Swinton it seems that period was quite considerable. Jackson played for the first team on 30 November 1901 when he travelled over the Pennines to meet Brighouse Rangers.

The following Saturday, 7 December, he should have taken the field over in Hull but did not! The local newspaper report of the game says that "the team was short of J. Jones that player having betaken himself to Wales for a holiday"

It must have been some holiday as it was not until 15 February 1902 before Jackson returned to the club in a reserve game against Runcorn 'A' at home. Once more there is confirmation of this from the local newspaper report which says: "... the front rank was strengthened by the inclusion of J. Jones who had not previously played since November 30."

There is an interesting little aside gleaned from the *Salford Reporter* which printed a preview of the match against Oldham on 1 March 1902 which read: "For the game with Oldham this afternoon the only change in the team which beat Salford on Saturday is the substitution of Jack Jones for G.R. Jones amongst the forwards."

What is known is that Jackson did not stay at the club much longer and the reason for that can only be speculated upon. It could well have been that he was coming to terms with the new game, attracting too much publicity and attention from his performances on the field. Were people more and more curious as to what his real identity was, knowing full well it was not Jones? Maybe he thought it was better to quit while ahead. There is one other interesting thing about his time at Swinton, during that season the club full-back was an ever present and so played in the same side as Jackson. Little did he or Jackson know that their paths were to cross once again some nine years or so in the future. Whatever the reasons, at the end of the 1901–02 season Jackson left Swinton, never to return.

He did seem to use information he may have picked up from listening to his team mates in order to manufacture a persona for each and every situation he found himself in from his rugby skills. On the other hand he could have just had a vivid imagination. He most certainly used this acquired knowledge to good effect when laying his trails of deception.

One thing not in dispute is that having left Swinton he returned to his 'new' roots, the Cornish ones down in Camborne. Even then things did not go in a simple and straight forward manner, but then nothing about Jackson at this time was simple or straightforward.

3. Camborne, Cornwall and Leicester

It seems that on his return from Manchester Jackson began playing once again for Camborne. There is unsubstantiated evidence that he had played for Camborne before 1900. Then for reasons which will become apparent, he suddenly switched his allegiance to Plymouth and he began to play for them. In 1904, playing as F.S. Jackson, he made a guest appearance for London Welsh against Plymouth, while the club was on a tour of the south west of England. It may well have been that following the game he was approached and induced to join Plymouth, much to the annoyance of Camborne. Such inducements broke the rugby union's rules of the time. What inducement, if any, the Plymouth club made to entice Jackson to move shall never be known, but he changed his allegiance and turned out for the Devon club. The switch of club may have involved some financial recompense, or was there another reason why Jackson wanted to move?

There is also evidence that suggests that he making spasmodic appearances for Swansea yet again, although the Swansea club say that they have no record of this. Further evidence suggests that around this time he occasionally made the trip up to Leicester and turned out for them, playing as Jackson. Was he juggling two personalities, Jackson, at Leicester and Plymouth and Gabe in Wales? Playing rugby union under an assumed name did not break the game's laws, and while such action was not common, it was not unheard of. Also, as most of the matches were not in a competition, it was not unusual for players to play as guests for different clubs, Leicester were an 'invitation' club anyway who recruited from other clubs.

The question that cannot be answered after all this time is how did Jackson get the time off work to travel from the south west to the midlands to play for Leicester? Jackson would have been paid his travel and hotel expenses by the club. Would he have made all that effort to play at Welford Road for nothing? Past experience of him suggests not.

Jackson was a very good player and wherever he played he stood out as a quality forward and goalkicker. He would also have stood out because of his size, he must have seemed like a giant of a man on the rugby pitch. It was only natural that more senior clubs would be interested in getting such a player to join their club. Equally, Jackson was beginning to interest the County selectors and in the 1902–03 season while with Camborne let it be known to the Cornwall selectors that as a 'Cornishman' he was available to represent the county if selected. They in turn were delighted to accept the services of such an experienced player.

Jackson only played 16 times for Cornwall, not a great number of county caps given that he played for the county around seven years or so. In that time the county played over 30 games, including friendly games and matches against the tourists from down under. Whatever conspired to cause it, Jackson missed the game against the touring All Blacks in 1905, the biggest game in the county's history up to that time. The game was played on Thursday 21 September and was staged at his old stomping ground Camborne. Did he not play for fear of a hostile reception from the Camborne supporters? It is more likely that he did not wish any photographs of himself to appear in the national newspapers and alert Swinton and others of his whereabouts.

The All Black tour, the first of its kind in this country, was attracting tremendous interest from both the public and the press. There would have been just too much attention focussed on that game for his liking. The question is what was he doing when he missed this and other county matches? Throughout his career he seems to have had a habit of going missing for two or three games on the trot before reappearing and carrying on as if nothing was amiss. These disappearances never have been adequately explained, but seemed to occur regularly during a season. There was a similar pattern while he was playing for Swinton.

However, having missed out on playing for Cornwall against the tourists he took the field against them for Leicester just nine days later. Perhaps he felt that this game would not attract the same level of publicity as the county game, it did, however, result in him being photographed. The New Zealanders defeated Leicester 28–0 and while for some time the fact that Jackson played in that game seems to have been 'lost' it is confirmed in a number of books published much later about that tour. Christopher Tobin in *The Original All-Blacks 1905–06* wrote: "…One of the Leicester forwards, Camborne born Fred Jackson, would tour New Zealand three years later with the Anglo-Welsh." This view is supported by Ron Palenski in *All-Blacks v Lions:* "Jackson had played for Leicester against the All-Blacks in 1905…."

The other notable thing is that *The Bystander* in October 1905 published a photograph of the game in which Jackson appeared. However, it shows him in such a position as to make it difficult for people to state for sure that he was the Jones who played for Swinton earlier. Jackson would have been able to claim that the photograph was much too vague for people to recognise his as Jones of Swinton.

The Cornwall team that played the Springboks in 1906.

The Cornwall team that beat Devon to win the 1908 South West Championship. Jackson is third from the right on the back row. He looks far from happy at being photographed. (Possibly this photograph caused his downfall but it is more likely it was the one in the *West Briton* just before the County Final)

There is yet another mystery surrounding Jackson in this period of his career. It has been possible to establish that he was playing for both Camborne and Plymouth from around 1902 through to 1905, but he then appears to disappear from the rugby scene completely. There is no reference to him playing after that period. Was he injured, taking a break from the game or perhaps work commitments prevented him playing? That shall probably never become known after all this time, but he does not seem to play again until he surfaces at Leicester.

His county appearances brought him to the attention of the more senior and fashionable clubs, including Leicester and around 1906 they began to invite him to turn out for them on a much more regular – if somewhat irregular – basis. This arrangement went on for some years. Leicester would have paid his expenses on these occasions, Would an employer have allowed a man to leave early on a Friday or miss work on a Monday as he would have had to in order to meet these playing commitments? Whatever payment arrangements Leicester made with him would certainly have been broken rugby union's professionalism rules because they would have constituted the 'broken time' payments that were one of the main causes of the split that led to the formation of the Northern Union.

So, towards the end of the 1904–05 season, Jackson appears to drop out of the rugby scene. He claimed in the pen picture published in the *Taranaki Herald* in 1908 that he captained Cornwall in 1903–04. This was untrue as that season the county was captained by Smith, a Falmouth player. However there seems to be very little else involving him during the 1905–6 season.

Jackson then joined Leicester on a permanent basis and turned out for the club and Cornwall reasonably regularly. That said even when at Leicester he would disappear for two or three games at a time. He very quickly became a firm favourite with the club's supporters in spite of these absences. All the evidence from newspaper reports suggest Jackson was one of the team's best forwards for Leicester with the added bonuses that he could kick goals and his kicking out of hand was quite prodigious.

He was also no slouch when it came to crossing the whitewash, but it did take him a while to settle. In his first full season for the club, 1906–07, he was the club's top points scorer. It was in his second season, 1907–08, that he seems to have set English rugby buzzing with excitement. He scored 14 tries that season, including three hat-tricks.

For a forward that was a considerable achievement back at the turn of the last century as it would be even today.

So how did he arrive at Leicester? In an article in the *Daily Chronicle* in June 1908, when the scandal over professionalism first was brought to the attention of the public, it said: "How the Leicester club were led to include F. Jackson in their team is a most interesting story. The *Daily Chronicle* Leicester correspondent has made exhaustive enquires from the most reliable sources and what appears to have happened was this: Jackson intimated that he would frequently be in Leicester, where he intended to settle down in a business career. He had been playing for Plymouth and Cornwall County in the same name, and he was selected and given a trial as a forward. He proved so capable a player that afterwards, for four seasons he played frequently for the side, although there were occasionally two or three matches in succession when he was not available. He proved a great favourite with the spectators and his massive figure and his curly black hair made him a most conspicuous figure on the side."

Facing allegations that could damage his club, there is no doubt that the Leicester secretary, Tom Crumbie, and others at the club were both covering their backs and desperately attempting a damage limitation exercise. The club was facing increasing pressure with regard to claims of professionalism. Had they let it be known that they had been bringing Jackson up from the south west to play then there is no doubt more questions about professionalism would been raised.

If the article is correct he seems to have used the same approach with Leicester as that he used with Swinton, in as much as he seems to have asked the club for a trial. The article makes no mention of the club inviting him to travel and play for them in the previous seasons.

Things were not all plain sailing at his new club even when he first joined them on a permanent basis at the beginning of the 1906–07 season. Rumours were beginning to circulate even then about Jackson and his professional past. The question of professionalism was still a controversial one within rugby union. The schism of 1895 and its aftermath had seen many clubs switch to the Northern Union code. The vast majority of these had been in Lancashire, Yorkshire, Cumberland and Cheshire, although the new code was starting to establish a base in South Wales. The people who had opposed professionalism before 1895 were still around and more determined than ever to keep rugby union pure and unsullied by professionalism. They also felt the need to stop the Northern Union code from extending its influence.

The very successful tour by the All Blacks in 1905–06 had been completed. However, while the tour made enormous profits for both the English and New Zealand unions, the Dominion pocketing around £12,000, a tremendous amount in 1906, all was not well. It had emerged that the tourists had received an allowance of three shillings (15p) per day while on tour. There were still many in the game who subscribed to the maxim 'if you cannot afford to play the game then don't play it'. Both the Scottish and Irish unions felt that by accepting such an allowance the players were professionals, more importantly the New Zealand union for paying such allowances were also guilty of professionalism and by association all New Zealand players must be regarded as being professional.

If there was a dispute at international level there were also problems at grassroots level. Many people felt that some clubs were guilty of playing players knowing that they had played Northern Union rugby. More importantly, many felt that clubs were themselves paying their top players generous 'expenses' or, even worse, were offering financial inducements to players to join their club. The issues from the 1905–06 New Zealand tour had not been resolved, which is why it was an Anglo-Welsh side that toured New Zealand in 1908.

The Midland Counties Rugby Union was particularly vigilant in suppressing professional activity of any kind. The Leicester club was coming under increasing scrutiny from many people and other clubs. There was a belief that Leicester were guilty of paying their players or at least enticing them to join the club from rival clubs. Their accounts had been under scrutiny for a number of years without any charges being laid against them. There was also the feeling that Leicester were playing players knowing that they had in the past played professionally.

There is a good deal of evidence that suggests that Leicester had become so powerful within the game that the authorities in London were reluctant to take them on. They clearly were aware that should Leicester switch allegiance to the rival code as was likely if the Rugby Union moved against them, then it could instigate another split within the game as catastrophic as the 1895 one. It appears that the authorities always came down on the side of the club in all the dealings and allegations made against it by others within the game. However, the Midland Counties were not prepared to sit back and do nothing and continued to push hard its anti-professional stance.

The Rugby Union's leadership realised that they needed to be seen to be taking action against professionalism of any kind, set up a sub-committee. That committee's remit was to investigate any allegations of professionalism that it received from players clubs or county unions, in fact from anyone who cared to approach it. However, the sub-committee proved to be very ineffectual and as shall be seen matters were to come to a head at the Rugby Union AGM in May 1908 when they were accused of failing to pursue claims of professionalism against players and clubs made to them.

Jackson himself came under intense scrutiny. His situation came to a head in December 1906 when he was referred to the professional sub-committee. There is no way of knowing just who actually brought him to the attention of the sub-committee, but it does not need a great deal of imagination to suppose it was the Midland Counties Union that did so. The charge was that he was a professional, having played for a Northern Union club earlier in his career. The suggestion was made that if the subcommittee were to get a photograph of Jackson then it would have no difficulty in proving Jackson's guilt. Getting such a photograph seems to have been beyond the sub- committee, or more accurately beyond its will and so no action was taken. What this suggests is that it was known that Jackson was John Jones of Swinton and it was this which had led to the referral. After all playing as Gabe would not at that time have infringed any laws on professionalism.

These facts were not revealed to the press or the public at the time, as was normal. After all, a player was innocent until proven guilty. Once again Leicester had come under scrutiny from the authorities and by some means or other managed to come away squeaky clean. It seemed that few were ever found guilty or even thoroughly investigated for that matter around this time. Once cleared, Jackson would have felt safe that his past was no longer going to be put under the same scrutiny again, but he was wrong.

When Jackson was sensationally recalled from the Anglo-Welsh tour of New Zealand in 1908 accused of professionalism, an article appeared in the *West Briton* newspaper in Cornwall. In the article a letter was included from a Mr Percy Adams, an Old Edwardian from Birmingham. In it he made a number of allegations, one of which confirmed what had happened to the allegations against Jackson: "His name and story were given to the Professional sub-committee in December 1906, as a define case for their enquiry. That committee were told that if they would produce a photograph of him, which it was impossible to get, then proof positive of his professionalism could be obtained. This offer the sub-committee treated with contempt and negligence."

In fairness to the committee photographs of Jackson around that time were practically non-existent. He had consistently shown a great deal of skill and ingenuity in avoiding the photographer's lens. There is even a group photograph of the Anglo-Welsh tourists in 1908 prior to their departure down under in which Jackson is nowhere to be seen. There was the photograph of him playing against the All-Blacks in 1905, but that seems not to have entered into the thoughts of the sub-committee for whatever reason.

The Swansea photographs of the period Jackson was supposed to be playing for them do not include him. The same is true in Neath and Llanelli. There were very few photographs of him when he represented Cornwall. Also, as will become apparent, Mr Adams had his own axe to grind. It was he who was to second the proposal put down by the Moseley club at the AGM in May 1908 on professionalism.

While on the surface nothing new seemed to be happening with regard to Jackson and the allegations of professionalism, underneath things were bubbling away. The Leicester club secretary, Tom Crumbie, having recruited Jackson to play for the club sought, in 1906, to get him selected for the Midlands County team. He proposed that Jackson would not be averse to switching allegiance from Cornwall to the Midlands should he be selected. He very quickly withdrew his proposal when it was made clear to him that the Midlands County had no desire to have Jackson represent them in the upcoming County Championships. They had taken notice of Jackson's referral to the professional subcommittee and were not willing to play him in their team. They also seemed to have some doubts with regard to his nationality! As we shall see following Crumbie's failed attempts, he was forced to admit that he knew Jackson was, he believed, Ivor Gabe.

On the field Jackson was fast becoming one of the foremost forwards in the English rugby scene. So well was he performing for his new club that people were beginning to talk about him representing England in the end of season international matches. The fact that the England selectors never came calling may well have had something to do with Jackson's referral to the professional sub-committee along with the Midlands Counties refusal to play him. It may well have been that they also believed from the available evidence that he was ineligible to represent them, not just because he was a professional, but because he was not English. Jackson at one time or another claimed to be Welsh as well as Cornish. Had they noted Crumbie's admission regarding the possibility that Jackson was Gabe? Given this situation still the Rugby Union refused to take action of any kind against Jackson other than refusing to select him for the national side. It does seem odd that they would flout their own laws, but it must also be remembered at this time Leicester seemed to be able to do and get away with far more than other clubs could.

Jackson had survived the inquiry into his professionalism and got on with his career. Perhaps he believed that he had 'escaped' further scrutiny and that the matter was now closed. Sadly, that proved not to be the case. The civil war over professionalism raging in the game was about to be stepped up a notch or two. Jackson's success continued at Leicester. He was the club's top points scorer and was playing as well as ever, perhaps better as he got used to playing in the upper echelons of the game. He also began to play more regularly for Cornwall.

As the 1907–08 season came to a climax all sorts of things were happening for Jackson. His great form on the football field and his point scoring ability caused the Anglo-Welsh selectors to begin to look at this forward who seemed to have ability to burn. There is no doubt that they were aware of the black cloud which hung over his head, but the selectors were on the horns of a dilemma. The Scottish and Irish Rugby Unions had reservations about the status of New Zealand players who had toured here in 1905–06, and thus refused to join in the tour in 1908.

The other problem for rugby union was that a young New Zealander by the name of Albert Baskerville had thrown the whole sport into turmoil. In 1907 he brought over to England a professional All-Black rugby squad, specifically to play the Northern Union brand of rugby. That tour had sparked off a revolution in Sydney which had resulted in the formation of the New South Wales Rugby League and on their return to their own country had resulted in the New Zealand Rugby League being born. This is confirmed by an article in the *Evening Post* in Wellington on the eve of the first match of the tour on 23 May 1908. The reporter stated of the tour: "...it is undertaken with a twofold objective. Firstly, to return the New Zealand visit of 1905... Secondly to help forward the amateur cause in New Zealand and Australia, a most praiseworthy undertaking indeed. Professionalism has taken a tremendous hold of the association game in recent years and it has occurred in some adventurous individuals in New Zealand as well as New South Wales that there is money in the rugby code if it be properly presented and popularised.

...The professional All-Blacks left their country unhonoured and unsung. Their return with an admittedly poor record is not likely to occasion any public rejoicing such as marked their predecessors. Still the professional seed has been sown. The New Zealanders were a success financially, the greed for gold may lead to an attempt to establish the Northern Union code in the Dominion."

The New Zealand Rugby Union, seeing the growth of the Northern Union game which was better suited to the way the game was played down under, sought to protect their own code from further erosion. To that end they approached the British unions with a view to the British Lions entering on a tour to both New Zealand and Australia. The hope was that such a tour would kill off the professional code in both countries, before it could develop a stronghold. They had noted the crowds in Sydney flocking to see the new code and the effect of that on New South Wales rugby union. They had no desire to be faced with a similar situation in their country. The tour, while not achieving what the authorities wanted was instrumental in Jackson's downfall.

When the tour was proposed the selectors began to view possible candidates for selection then the double bombshell hit them. Both the Scots and the Irish authorities declared that for any of their players to go to New Zealand and play against players who were getting expenses would be tantamount to playing against professionals and they themselves would be professionalised. They forbad any of their players from accept a place on the tour, causing huge problems for the Lions selectors. However, New Zealand was adamant that the tour was vital if the game was to survive the attack from the Northern Union code down under and begged that the tour go ahead.

The selectors a little reluctantly decided to support the New Zealand request and hastily began to organise an Anglo-Welsh tour party. Both the English and Welsh unions had no inhibitions about their players travelling down under to play the game. Given that the number of players available to them had been effectively halved they decided that Jackson was simply too good a player to be left at home, despite the ongoing problems and allegations associated with charges of professionalism. They were not particularly bothered if he was Welsh or English as whatever the case he was eligible for selection. There was also the possibility that had he not been selected questions would have been asked of the authorities as to just why Jackson was not in the team. Overall, they probably thought it was better to pick the player and risk any consequences rather than not and come under scrutiny. It was a decision which would eventually bring matters to a head for Jackson and end his rugby union career. It would not do much for the good name of the game either.

A picture published in the *Bystander* in October 1905 when Leicester played the touring All Blacks. Jackson is in the striped shirt with his hands on his hips. It would, however, be difficult to prove this was him and was probably why it was not used to prove he was Jones, the Swinton professional player.

The Cornwall team before playing Durham in 1908.
This photograph in *The West Briton* on the Thursday before the County
Championship Final probably led to Jackson's downfall

Cornwall versus Durham, County Championship Final in March 1908.
Jackson is at the back of the line out with his hands on his hips.

4. County champion and tourist

As was the norm back then when such a tour was being organised the selection committee set up to choose the squad met at regular intervals and discussed the merits of various players. Once they were agreed that a particular player would be a suitable candidate for a place on that tour they would approach him and offer a place in the tour party. Not all players would have wanted to be away from home for such a long period of time, a tour of this nature in 1908 would mean a player being away from home for up to seven months or more. Equally, some players simply could not afford to be away from home and work for the length of time a tour would take.

The consequence of this was that members of the tour party were announced in an ad hoc manner over a period of time. As and when a player or players accepted the invitation to join the tour then their name was announced to the national press. So it was that on 22 February 1908 it was announced in the press that a number of players, one of which was Fred Jackson, had accepted a place on the Anglo-Welsh tour to New Zealand and Australia. If Jackson thought the problems of the allegations of professionalism had been permanently swept under the carpet as a result of his selection he was about to find out that some people were intent on ripping up the carpet to reveal what lay beneath it. There can be little doubt that certain people in the Midland Counties Union would have been infuriated by his selection and were determined to do something about it!

The other interesting aspect of the announcement was that Jackson was happy to accept a place on the tour. Given that there is little information on how he earned a living the question has to be asked, how could he support himself for such a long period without working? Clearly he would have had a roof over his head, been fed and given some expenses while on tour, but it seems that he could abandon whatever occupation he had. Either he was in a comfortable well paid job and had an enlightened employer who was happy to give in six or seven months leave of absence, or he was sufficiently wealthy to be able to stand the loss of income while supporting himself over that period. All the available evidence would suggest that he was not a mining engineer as he had claimed while at Camborne. So just what did he do for a living that would allow him to go away on a seven month rugby tour? Certainly all research regarding this issue has failed to turn up any evidence of just what Jackson did to earn money.

It is difficult to believe that Jackson could have funded himself solely from rugby. Around that period most Northern Union clubs would be paying their players around £2/10 (£2.50 in today's money) for a win. If this was the norm then it is difficult to believe that Leicester or Plymouth would be paying any more. That money would not be sufficient for Jackson to live on and still travel as he did.

Having accepted a place on the tour, Jackson simply got on with doing what he did best, play rugby. As outlined before, he was having great success with Leicester. In the County Championship he had helped Cornwall reach their first final, where they played Durham at Redruth in front of a sell-out crowd.

It had been a long hard road to the County Championship final for Cornwall and the quest had begun way back on 2 November 1907. It was covered by *The Times* newspaper. On that day Cornwall had made the trip up to Taunton to meet Somerset where they came away with the spoils 25–6. According to *The Times* the win against Somerset which started the journey was not as comprehensive as the score line suggested. Just five days later they were on the move once again, this time to Plymouth, Jackson's old club, where Devon brought them down to earth, winning 17–8. Cornwall then faced Gloucestershire in their final game, this time at home in Redruth, and ran out easy winners by 34–10. Jackson converted a try to bring Cornwall back into the match they were at the time losing 10–0. The Cornishmen came good in the second half. Back then the championship was played out as three divisions. The winners of the Northern division, as they were considered to be the strongest rugby area in the country, would play in the final the winners of the tie between the South East champions and the South West champions.

Cornwall, Gloucestershire and Devon tied for the South West title and were forced to play off. This time home advantage went to Cornwall and at Redruth they managed a reversal of fortune turning over Devon 21–3. Having lost their first encounter with Devon the play-off against them took place in front of a partisan crowd. It was reported that "... their meeting with Devon at Redruth yesterday, aroused more than ordinary interest, and a crowd of about 5,000 people watched the game..." There is a photograph of that winning team against Devon and Jackson is clearly seen not looking very happy at being in the picture. The victory against Devon meant they again had to travel up to Gloucester knowing a victory would take them through to the play-off against the South East champions. In a much harder game this time they came away with a 15–3 victory and a place in the play-off against Middlesex. Once again Cornwall and Jackson would have home advantage and it proved to be decisive as they beat Middlesex by 19–3 to set up a County Championship Final against Durham, the Northern Champions. Middlesex had given as good as they got in the first half until Jackson and his pack gained the upper hand. It was reported that "…Jose who played finely all through, gained a try, but later Sibree scored for Middlesex, the score at the interval being a try each. After changing ends the Cornish forwards dominated the game, and further tries were gained by Milton (two), Bennett and Davey, two being converted by Jackson…"

On the day of the Final Cornwall proved to be too strong and on 28 March 1908 in front of 17,000 fans crammed into the tiny ground at Redruth, they defeated Durham 17–3. In doing so they scored four tries, Jackson adding a conversion, and the crowd was in no doubt who was the man-of-the-match. As the game ended the crowd swarmed onto the pitch to celebrate the first ever win in the County Championship by the Cornishmen and to carry off shoulder high the man they deemed responsible for the success, Fred Jackson. The final against Durham had been the first for the Cornishmen and according to *The Times* it was a game they were not expected to win: "…Durham, who have won their way into the final tie on nine successive occasions were generally regarded as the most formidable opponents whom Cornwall could have been called upon to face. The reason is simple. In point of personnel the Durham side has altered but little for several seasons, so that the Durham men have had considerable experience as 'Finalist'. They enjoy, too, a well-deserved reputation as determined fighters, and a side who are difficult to beat…"

The county had the added incentive of knowing that as county champions they had earned the right to represent the country at the upcoming Olympic Games to be held later in the year. Sadly Jackson would be in New Zealand instead of plying his trade for Cornwall at the Olympic Games.

In a career which had at that time spanned some 10 years or more, there can be little doubt that winning the County Championship would have been the highlight of Jackson's career so far. The chance to tour New Zealand and Australia would have been 'the icing on the cake'.

It was at the County Championship final that Jackson made a fatal mistake. In the euphoria he allowed himself to be photographed along with the rest of the victorious Cornwall team by a newspaper photographer prior to the match. In reality he probably could not get out of being in the team photograph. It was a picture that was to have dire consequences for Jackson and in truth change the whole course of his life.

That photograph of the team and the county officials was actually published in the local Cornwall paper the *West Briton*. It was published on the Thursday as the final was played on the Saturday. Somehow or other a copy of that photograph found its way up to officials at the Midland Counties. It is not beyond the bounds of possibility that knowing Cornwall were to contest the final Midland Counties officials would have travelled to Redruth under the guise of watching the match. They would however have been looking closely at the local paper for any photograph(s) of the Cornish team in the hope that they would obtain an image of Jackson that they knew would most certainly identify him as Gabe or Jones, the former Swinton Player. They were not disappointed as the *West Briton* duly obliged. It was the opportunity that they had been waiting for and they were not going to let it pass. They busily set about using the photograph to launch an attack on both Jackson and Leicester. While the ammunition was being manufactured by the Midland Counties it was to be the Moseley club that would be chosen to fire it.

So the season ended on a high for Jackson, even though he would eventually miss out on the Olympic Games he was on his travels once more and this time further than South Africa. The tourists gathered together in London on the Thursday prior to sailing and in the evening attended a dinner hosted by the New Zealand Consul to the United Kingdom, Mr Wray-Palliser. Wray-Palliser was also the New Zealand Rugby Union representative on the RFU executive. On Friday 3 April the tour party gathered at Howard Hotel in Norfolk Street in London for a farewell breakfast and when the speeches were completed it was down to business. The tourists went aboard the Shaw-Savill Lines' steamer Athenic which would take them to New Zealand.

As the ship steamed out into the English Channel neither Jackson nor the rest of the party had any idea what was about to unfold at home while they were away. Nor were they aware just how rapidly events would move and the consequences they would have.

While the Athenic and Jackson were sailing south an article in the *Salford Reporter* on 25 April would have set alarm bells ringing had he seen it. It was a letter sent to the newspaper and was brief and most certainly to the point: "A correspondent writes, I have seen a paper containing portraits of the men who have gone out to New Zealand under the auspices of the Rugby Union and I recognised that of the one time Swinton forward, J. Jones, who by some was dubbed the 'mysterious Jones'. From Swinton Jones went to Plymouth and in connection with the rugby union team of that town acquired county honours. On leaving Plymouth he found refuge so I am informed by one who knew him well at Swinton, but is now settled in Leicester in the name of Fred Jackson."

So the connection had once again been made between Jackson and Jones and the proposition that they were one and the same, one professional, one amateur. It would have been manna from heaven for one midland club.

The Athenic continued on its journey and an article in the *Otago Witness* in New Zealand on 8 July provides an insight into the 'goings on' on aboard. In his football notes the New Zealand correspondent 'Dropkick' wrote: "The *London Sportsman's* special correspondent with the English team writing from Cape Town says a most amusing incident of the voyage to date was enacted on Wednesday 15 April. Father Neptune for the day in the person of Jackson, ably assisted by Edgar Morgan, Kyrke and Green demanded the usual victims. As so many were crossing the line for the first time lots were drawn, to see who should be sacrificed to the 'The Gods of the Ocean. The unfortunates were, Gibbs, Thomas, Vassall, Griffiths, Chapman and J.L. Williams. At 12 noon all were assembled on the lower deck. Here Father Neptune tenderly fondling a wooden razor some two foot long calmly stood behind a chair awaiting his victims. His chief assistant nearby bent over a large bucket containing a curious pink looking lather which proved to be a mixture of treacle, flour and cochineal and with a large paint brush in hand awaited his victims."

This was the ceremony of 'crossing the line' which is still carried out today on people crossing the equator for the first time. The interesting point is that Father Neptune was the role taken by Fred Jackson which suggests he had crossed the line before. That being the case it would support the claim that he had spent some time in South Africa earlier in his life, as he claimed, in interviews in 1901 while with Swinton and in 1908 on the dockside at Wellington when he was recalled from the tour.

On the rugby side of things Jackson's reputation as a player was travelling before him. On 16 April the *Nelson Evening Mail* in anticipation of the upcoming tour wrote of him: "Jackson (Leicester) of the Anglo-Welsh team is a fine scoring forward, and a great goalkicker. His latest achievement in this line was to kick seven goals in succession. It would take Messenger or Freddie Jones all their time to beat that." (Both 'Dally' Messenger the Australian and Freddie Jones of

New Zealand were both notable goalkickers of the time.) It was praise indeed from a rugby fraternity that generally was quite critical of players other than their own.

Meanwhile, back in London, just two days after the tourists' departure the newspapers published the agenda for the forthcoming Rugby Union AGM. Tucked away on the agenda was a motion to be proposed by the Midlands club Moseley. It read: "That this meeting is not satisfied that veiled professionalism does not exist in the Rugby Union, and view with alarm the attitude of the Rugby Union Committee toward the whole question."

Just why the Moseley club chose to put the motion forward at this time can only be speculated upon after so long. Perhaps they had discovered Jackson's earlier referral to the professional sub-committee, although they must surely have been aware of it. More likely they were disappointed with the findings as a whole that seemed to emanate from the professional sub-committee.

In particular there would have been a good deal of rivalry between themselves and the successful Leicester club who had been accused of professionalism but been cleared after a somewhat flimsy investigation by the authorities. That would have annoyed officials at Moseley who felt Leicester undermining the amateur ethos which the Midlands Counties vehemently supported.

So the motion from Moseley was set to be debated at the end of May at the Rugby Union AGM. In all probability it must have been thought that the motion would simply die a death and the status quo continue within the game. What was not known was just what the Moseley club and the Midland Counties Union officials had managed to achieve with that simple team photograph of the Cornwall team which contained Jackson's image. They kept their activities very close to their chest about the photograph. They would, however, reveal all as and when needed at the forthcoming AGM. For now they would keep their powder dry.

Moseley's action may have been triggered by, or more likely had triggered the article mentioned earlier in the *Salford Reporter*? One thing was certain, Jackson was to come under threat and at a time when he could do little or nothing about it.

On board ship the tour party continued to try to keep fit and enjoy the journey down to New Zealand. Most of the players did not train because they felt that to do so would be against the amateur ethos which they supported. Writing in *All-Blacks v Lions* Ron Palenski said of the tourists: "The Anglo-Welsh team eventually selected was deridingly middle class and determinedly amateur in spirit – to the extent that they eschewed shipboard training on the way to New Zealand on the grounds that gentlemen who played the game for its own sake had no reason to prepare for it."

On 18 May they arrived in New Zealand and proceeded to prepare for the first game of the tour. First there were the official ceremonies. A welcoming ceremony had been organised at Wellington Town Hall, such was the excitement about the visit that some 3,000 people came to greet the tourists. The Town Hall was decked in union flags and banners saying "England expects that every man will do his duty." That duty done it was down to the preparation required if they were to get the better of the New Zealand teams they would face. However, training seemed to take second place to holiday making by a good many of the tourists; they had travelled to the other side of the world and were going to enjoy themselves even if the rugby took a back seat.

On Saturday 23 May they took the field against Wairarapa at the Memorial Ground in Masterton, looking resplendent in their broad red and white hooped shirts. Jackson was to watch the action from the stand as he was not selected for the match. It seemed that on the previous Thursday it had been decided to play a trial game during the training session. During the course of that match Jackson along with another player, Chapman, a threequarter, picked up an injury that would keep him out of the first two tour games. The home side proved no match for the tourists who ran out winners 17–3. It was, however, not a great performance by the tourists which was to be expected because just a week earlier they had still been at sea. The press were not so forgiving and claimed that 'They won't beat the best provinces' and that 'The strong provinces will "out them"'. Their predictions were to prove somewhat prophetic as the tour progressed.

The following Wednesday the tourists returned to Wellington to play the Wellington team. It was a game which brought them down to earth with a bang and made very clear just what they were up against on this tour. Jackson was still not selected to play. Wellington won 19–13. The tourists' cause was not helped much when their full-back, Jackett, was injured while trying to prevent a score and had to leave the field for a time. In New Zealand an injured player was allowed to be replaced and so in addition to selecting the 15 players generally an 'emergency back and forward' were also selected. The Rugby Union rules in England did not allow this. So it was that the tourists never took advantage of this local rule and played on with 14 men while Jackett received lengthy treatment. By half-time they were 16–0 down.

The second half saw them fight back and as the match was coming to a close they had clawed their way back into it at 16–13. However a try by the home side at the death saw the Wellington team take the spoils

Jackson would have been disappointed; first with the defeat, and second that he was still sitting on the sidelines not having started a game. That was about to change, but little did he know that back home in England the following day, a train of events would be set in motion that would result in him sitting on the rugby union sidelines permanently. Having been given the word that he was to play in the next game, he simple knuckled down to serious training prior to making his debut for the Anglo-Welsh tourists.

Jackson was taking the tour seriously, unlike some of his colleagues, because he fully intended to maintain the reputation that had preceded him to New Zealand, one of being one of the top forwards in the English game.

5. The fateful 1908 RFU AGM

On Thursday 28 May at the Holborn Restaurant in London the Rugby Football Union AGM opened and started its business. A steady stream of non contentious matters was discussed and the meeting wore on. It then came to the motion being proposed by the Moseley club. Opinion among the delegates was divided over the proposal. Some felt that the motion was nothing more than a disgraceful attack upon the professionalism sub-committee in particular and the rugby union's leadership in general, while others felt the claims were justified and the sub-committee was doing little or nothing to root out growing professionalism within the game. The RFU President, Mr C. A. Crane, called on the Moseley club to speak to their motion regarding veiled professionalism existing within the game and that the attitude of the authorities to it was a cause for some alarm.

Mr Byrne from Moseley was due to propose the motion, but was suffering from a heavy cold which affected his ability to speak. He therefore called upon Mr Godfrey to read his speech. His basic argument was that the union needed to decide if they intended to make popular the game of rugby under any and every code, or if they should restrict it entirely to amateurs. He went on to suggest that in his opinion the committee had not truly addressed the question of veiled professionalism within the game. The implication was that the professionalism sub-committee was simply brushing allegations regarding professionalism under the carpet rather than rooting out the perpetrators. To be fair to Moseley, the sub-committee never seemed to take any allegation brought to it very seriously and little or no action seems to have ever been taken. That was about to change.

Warming to his task, Godfrey went on to quote instances when clubs had committed irregularities, paid expenses and induced players to leave one club and join another and no action had been forthcoming from the sub-committee when such matters had been referred to them. When he had inquired of the sub-committee why this was he had been told only that it was of little use inquiring into the claims as they were so 'shadowy'. For that reason Mr Byrne's speech claimed that the sub-committee appointed to inquire into the subject of professionalism had failed to do its duty. Shadowy or otherwise, claims should have been investigated and reported upon and they had not been. It seems Godfrey then warmed even more to his task.

The Anglo-Welsh in New Zealand, Jackson is third from the left on the
second row wearing the white waistcoat.
(Photo: *The British Tourists in Maoriland* by R.A. Barr)

He began to state specific instances which he considered demanded inquiry and nothing had been done. He went on to name players and then dropped his first bombshell. He claimed that one of the players presently in New Zealand with the Anglo-Welsh tourists was a professional and that he had actually played for a Northern Union club, something expressly forbidden under the present rules on professionalism. Having proposed the motion on behalf of Moseley, Mr Godfrey resumed his seat in a room which had fallen silent, some delegates angry with the sub-committee, others indignant at the perceived attack on the sub-committee. It then fell to Mr Percy Adams from the Old Edwardians club in Birmingham to second the motion. (This gentleman appears in Jackson's story again.)

He was quick to point out in seconding the motion that it should in no way be seen as a vote of censure on the sub-committee, although it is hard to see how the motion could be interpreted in any other way. On the contrary the motion only sought to awaken it to a sense of its responsibilities. Adams went on to assert that in his view the commission had started out with the belief that veiled professionalism did not exist in the game. However, the commission's own report proved that it did. In his opinion the commission was 'a solemn and expensive farce.' Like Mr Byrne he went into greater detail of irregularities which had been referred to the sub-committee and on which they had taken no action.

36

While Adams was making these allegations, the mood of the meeting was swiftly changing and polarising further. Those supporting the motion were incensed at what they saw as the inactivity of the sub-committee while those opposed saw Adams words as a personal affront to the Rugby Union. The meeting was in danger of getting out of hand when the sub-committee chairman, Mr Call, stood and reminded all present that the sub-committee would take evidence from any source and such evidence was treated in the strictest confidence.

Obviously, being to some extent forewarned he proceeded to address many of the cases that Byrne and Adams had quoted and stated that in the majority of them the evidence given to the sub-committee was both contradictory and unreliable. He ended by saying that the commission had come to the conclusion that after sifting through all the evidence on individuals and examining the accounts of all the clubs referred to them that veiled professionalism did not exist. It must be said it was not the strongest defence of the sub-committee's stance on dealing with evidence forwarded to it. Perhaps Mr Call felt that there was no need to defend the work done because the meeting would support of his stance. This had been the case in most situations when the sub-committee had arrived at a decision, the full committee of the rugby union had simply rubber stamped it and the counties had gone along with the decisions reluctantly or otherwise.

Once the meeting was thrown open for discussion on the motion, Leicester secretary Tom Crumbie was the first to speak and defended his club. Leicester had been suspected for some time, not without good reason, of playing fast and loose with the payment of players and playing players knowing they had been professional in the past. They also had a history of inducing players to leave their club and move to Leicester to play their rugby, something forbidden by the rules. He argued that the club had provided their account books for inspection by the sub-committee and they had proved to be satisfactory. The question is just how closely did the sub-committee scrutinise those books – they had a history of believing what clubs told them and supporting the actions of club officials. Also, available evidence suggests that Leicester seemed to have an uncanny ability to deflect any and all criticism made of the club and to have the ear of the rugby union's leading officials.

As has already been seen, Crumbie was at best economical with the truth and at worse lying about Leicester's activities. In defence of the club, he even said that in the previous 10 years the club had donated around £10,000 to various local charities, along with providing around

£200 every year to the development of local junior rugby in the area. What that had to do with professionalism is not really clear, but what it did do was quickly throw up a smoke screen around the whole issue. It was a good example of Crumbie being quick to occupy what he saw as the 'moral high ground' on this matter. It is obvious that there was a good deal of ill feeling between the Leicester and Moseley clubs. Maybe the latter resented the success the former enjoyed on the field. Perhaps also they resented what they saw as Leicester flouting the rules with seeming impunity given the powerful position the club held. Maybe these were the issues as much as the matter of professionalism that had led Moseley to drafting the motion in the first instance.

It would appear from reports of the meeting that after Crumbie had sat down the representatives from those unions and clubs under scrutiny wanted a say in their own defence. Also, those organisations not under suspicion wished to comment on the motion and put forward their views. For Devon, Mr Finch repudiated the claims that had been made (presumably by Byrne and Adams) against Devon clubs and invited the two gentlemen to come to Devon and carry out their own inquiries as the Devon union had done. It is notable that Jackson should transfer his allegiance from that part of the world to Leicester that seemed also to have been cited many times for professionalism. On the other hand, the Cheshire representative, Mr Thorpe, was outraged and stated in his opinion the charges made by Mr Byrne and Mr Adams were, 'of too shadowy a nature to be acted upon'. He went on to say that in his opinion the motion was tantamount to a vote of no confidence in the sub-committee.

However, Moseley were not going to back down and it was at this point that Mr Godfrey got to his feet once more and, reading from Mr Byrne's notes, dropped the second and biggest bombshell onto the meeting. He produced a signed affidavit and proceeded to read it to the assembled members. It was from the Swinton Northern Union club and was to the effect that one of the players presently in New Zealand with the Anglo-Welsh tour who had been referred to earlier, namely Frederick Stanley Jackson, was in the opinion of the Swinton club officials the same player whom they had signed and who had played for them under the name of John R. Jones back in the 1901–02 season.

Their claim was made on the basis of the photograph of the victorious Cornwall team at the recent County Championship final. The professionalism sub-committee back in 1906, when Jackson had been referred to them, had been unable or unwilling to seek to obtain a photograph of Jackson. In all probability that photograph or a copy of it had been supplied to the Swinton club by officials from Moseley, or by the Midland Counties officials. The upholders of amateurism were quite prepared to work with the Swinton Northern Union club, the enemy as many saw them, if it suited their own purposes. It was obvious that having obtained a photograph of Jackson, they were going to use it to the full in their attempts to bring Leicester down.

In the opinion of the Moseley club this was positive proof that Jackson and Jones were one and the same and therefore Jackson was a professional. The inference was that if Moseley could find such evidence why could the sub-committee not have done the same back in December 1906? The other inference was that the Leicester club knew full well that Jackson was Jones – the professional player, and so the club also was guilty of professionalism

The President of the RFU, Mr Crane, along with many others, was stunned at the news and was even more surprised when the chairman at the AGM having called for a vote on the Moseley motion announced the results. He stated that while 38 delegates had voted for the motion, 48 had voted against and therefore the motion was defeated. It seems many delegates were not prepared to believe the word of a professional Northern Union club even though it had the backing of the law of the land, such was the antagonism that existed between the two codes. It could well have been the case also that many delegates were fully aware of the wider implications of censuring Leicester. The Leicester club were delighted to escape from possible serious censure while Crane, the union's president, would later resign in disgust that Leicester had not been thrown out of rugby union for professionalism.

The furore caused by the allegations at the meeting would simply not go away and try as they might, the sub- committee and the RFU could not brush it under the carpet. The newspapers had got hold of the story and began to make great play about the row over professionalism within the game. They also latched onto the Jackson/Gabe mystery that had by now entered the public domain. With what seemed to be an open secret within the game now out in the open, more and more people came forward, including club officials and players, to offer new information, buoyed by news of the events at the AGM being made public. Mr Byrne, having now found his voice, said that a player called Matthews from the Leicester club had earlier signed a contract for the Hull NU club Hull and continued to say that Jackson was the John R. Jones that had played for the Swinton NU club.

It also became common knowledge within the game that Leicester were fully aware that Jackson was really Ivor Gabe as they admitted to the professional sub-committee back in December 1906, an admission the sub-committee never made public, even at the AGM. Many felt that if they knew Jackson was Gabe then it was not stretching a point too far to say they knew also that he was John R. Jones the Swinton professional player. Leicester still maintained their innocence, but did admit that their player Matthews had signed a form for Hull FC, a Northern Union club, on 24 January 1899, but had received no payment and never played for the Hull club, and at that time this was not a breach of the RFU's rules. In Leicester's defence they argued that they had not broken any rules in playing him in 1908.

It was becoming more difficult to suppress the knowledge that Jackson's real name could in fact be Gabe, as Crumbie had been forced to admit way back in 1906, but which had not been made public. What was even more damning was the claim that if Jackson was Gabe then he was Welsh, not English. Even more surprising was that the newspapers started to refer to Jackson as 'Gabe the well-known Swansea player'. This inference supported the fact that he was Welsh. It also backed the belief that the England selectors knew of the Welsh connection and therefore refused to select him for the national side, notwithstanding the allegations that he was a professional.

Still the authorities continued to try to defend the indefensible and a past RFU president, Mr Thorpe, stoutly defended the sub-committee. He said that their reports had always been subject to very careful analysis and accepted by the full RFU committee. This was clearly not the case as generally the full committee always supported the finding of its sub-committee on professionalism without any further investigation. He went on to say that if Mr Adams or anyone else had evidence that Jackson's status was in doubt they should have sent word to the relevant officials and not allowed him to go out to New Zealand. The Moseley club officials could have argued that they had done this, and so had the people who had submitted Jackson's name to the sub-committee back in December 1906. The Midland Counties Union had refused to select Jackson to play for them, because they believed him to have played as a professional. Leicester, however, were sticking to their story that they knew nothing of Jackson's past.

While all of this was going on in England, Jackson was preparing to make his debut for the Anglo-Welsh team to play Otago in Dunedin on Saturday 1 June. Even as he prepared for that match more people were coming forward and making more allegations about him, which would eventually bring him down.

6. The story breaks

At 3pm on Saturday 29 May, the day after the AGM back in London, Jackson took the field at Carisbrook in Dunedin to make his debut in international rugby. The Anglo-Welsh team were playing Otago and the result did not auger well for the visitors as they lost again 9–6, this after leading 6–3 at half-time. The match report says that the game was played mainly in the forwards and that the tourists were more than a match for the home pack for most of the game. It was a lack of fitness that let the visitors down and in the last quarter of the match the Otago pack got the upper hand and managed to score the winning try late in the game. The press seemed to take a favourable view to Jackson, one reporter feeling that with regard to the forwards who represented the tourists: "Jackson was the most prominent and invariably headed the Britishers in their dribbling rushes."

The press were already getting their knives out over the Anglo-Welsh team's play. It was felt that while they were holding their own in these early games, particularly in the forward play, they tended to fade in the latter part of the game. The team's lack of training and preparation compared to their hosts was showing. Given the amateur ethos existing at the time in England it was not surprising. Teams tended to train twice a week and even for 'big' matches generally speaking the players would assemble on the day of the match.

When they reached New Zealand they were meeting sides that trained hard and had been brought together for perhaps three or four days in a training camp, prior to the match. Such behaviour would have been considered 'professional' back home; usually the international side would only meet up on the morning of a game.

The other complaint levelled at the tourists was their attitude on the field. It was felt they were not playing at the same intensity as the home teams, having this "play the game for the game's sake attitude", rather then playing to win. The tourists for their part felt that the hosts were far too competitive in their approach to the game. As Ron Palenski put it: "From the outset the tourists developed a strong animosity towards the ferocious competitiveness of New Zealand teams and the fanaticism of their supporters, who seemed to treat the games as something akin to a 'religion'."

The feeling of the press was that in the tougher games to come the tourists would have problems. One player who was not singled out for criticism by the New Zealand reporters was Jackson, who they felt

41

played the game in the same spirit as the home players did. In other words he played hard and played to win.

The same reporter writing of the Otago game summed up the British approach when he wrote: "Condition, a prime factor in rugby, played an important part in today's struggle for supremacy, the Britishers have not yet settled into their stride and they are not keyed up to the desperate struggle which the match against Otago proved."

The *Otago Witness* on 3 June published a photograph of the tourist team prior to the kick-off. The players were all in their playing kit and wearing scarves and blazers and while the picture is on the dark side Jackson is clearly seen and once again looks far from happy.

For the most part Jackson had acquitted himself well in his first outing and the selectors must have thought so too, for he was selected to play on the following Wednesday. The tourists were to play Southland and it would give Jackson the opportunity to cement a place in the side which was to play New Zealand in the first test. However, back home things were now moving at an ever increasing pace. The AGM and all of the follow-on revelations from clubs and players reported by the newspapers and also to the professional sub-committee, had now placed Jackson in the firing line.

People who had previously kept their own counsel now felt happy to make their own claims to the sub-committee about Jackson. More worrying for his future in rugby union was that new claims were being made and substantiated, in particular that Jackson was none other than the Swansea forward Gabe. Players and club officials came forward to say that they knew that Jackson of Leicester was none other than Gabe who was a Swansea player and they had played against him or seen him while playing against Swansea. It now seemed clear to all that there were at least three aliases he had used, Jackson, Gabe and Jones.

The professional sub-committee were coming under enormous pressure, particularly from the Midlands Counties Union officials, to take decisive action on this issue. The Moseley club felt that their accusations had been proven and so were justified and they also wanted action, feeling that such action would bear them out. After all they must have felt their reputation had taken a battering most unfairly. Either the RFU had to clear the player after careful consideration of all the evidence or declare him to be in breach of the laws about professionalism. The newspapers were also increasing the pressure on the RFU by keeping the Jackson story on the boil.

The professionalism sub-committee continued to gather evidence and information about the matter and announced they would make their deliberations known to the RFU committee when they had completed their investigations. Possibly they were stalling to receive some guidance from the RFU leaders as to what was the best way forward, and maybe hoping the furore would die down. After all, the player in question was about to play for a team representing his country, be it Wales or England, no one knew for sure. However, it did not really matter as quite fortuitously he was to play for the Anglo-Welsh tourists.

Another equally important issue was the position of the Leicester club. In 1898 the RFU had compromised with the Welsh Football Union over allegations of professionalism against Arthur Gould, this avoiding a split that could have seen that union join the Northern Union. If Leicester were to be forced out of the RFU, they would be welcomed with open arms by the Northern Union code. No one knew just where that could lead, as other clubs could follow them. Had the RFU lost Leicester, their biggest and best supported club, to the Northern Union, it could have offered the NU a chance to expand into the midlands, and other areas of the country where there had been issues around professionalism, such as the south west and South Wales, could have followed. The RFU, which had already been weakened by the formation of the NU, could have been left as a rump, with the strongest areas of the game affiliated to the NU.

At the other side of the world the tourists were gaining their second victory of the tour, beating Southland 14–8. They made hard work of it having to come from 8–0 down to secure the win. Jackson was entrusted with the goalkicking duties and duly obliged by converting the two tries the visitors scored, while a Jackett drop-goal, in those days worth four points, completed the scoring. It also seems that in the second half Jackson showed that he was no slouch when it came to kicking out of hand because, according to the match reports, he constantly pinned the Southland team deep in their own half of the field with his booming touch finders and then made a nuisance of himself in the subsequent line-out.

He was at times controlling the game in a way not really seen back home and the New Zealanders appreciated his good play. He was quickly becoming a big favourite with the New Zealand supporters. All-in-all he was making it difficult for the selectors not to play him in the upcoming test match at the weekend.

On Saturday 6 June Fred Jackson made his international match debut against the might of New Zealand in front of 19,000 spectators at Dunedin. It was not the start to an international career he would have wanted. If the tourists thought they had a chance of winning the test match, that hope faded very rapidly. The spectators saw the All Blacks take the game by the scruff of the neck and gain a command they would never relinquish. All of the predictions the press had been making and all of the allegations they had levelled at the tourists proved to be correct. The All Blacks were relentless and ruthless in their pursuit of victory. By half-time they were leading 21–0 and cruising to victory; there was to be no way back for the visitors.

The second half saw the tourists score what was adjudged to be the best try of the game through Gibbs and Jackson stepped up to add the conversion. The final result was a 32–5 win for the All Blacks. Jackson was judged by many to be the best of the Anglo-Welsh forwards, but he would have still been very disappointed.

It was a harsh lesson for the visitors who came face-to-face with the way the game was played in New Zealand. There the object of the game was to win, nothing less was acceptable. The visitors were still in the frame of mind that the playing of the game was what mattered, not the winning. The home players, however, were quite happy to play up to the rules and occasionally beyond them if it meant winning the game. Also, as the press were now beginning to point out more and more frequently, the visitors seemed to be in the country on holiday first and to play the game second. It was going to take a massive effort to turn the tour around and they would not be helped by events in England which were rapidly coming to a head and would make a large impact on the tourists.

Just four days after the test match the squad travelled to Timaru, to play South Canterbury, with the players attempting to get the tour back on an even keel. They did so with a 12–6 victory in front of around 9,000 supporters, but the local press was still unimpressed with the quality of play. On the Saturday they faced the Canterbury side in Christchurch and this time there were over 15,000 crammed into the Lancaster Park ground. The home supporters had come hoping for a win and they were not disappointed; the visitors went down by 13–8 in a hard fought game. Jackson, who was rested for the match, watched from the stand.

It was, however, not the result the tourists wanted or for that matter needed. It was not the result the New Zealand union officials wanted as well, because they could see the supporters staying away if they felt there was not going to be a close contest from the visitors. Cracks were beginning to show in their ranks and they were beginning to criticise the referees and their interpretation of the rules. It was a sure sign they were under increasing pressure to perform and feeling it as well.

The tour, however, had to go on and the following Wednesday, 17 June, the team had travelled to Greymouth where they played a West Coast and Buller selection. Once more there was a large crowd in attendance, between 5,000 and 6,000. It was not a good performance by any means, but the tourists won 22–3. Jackson was restored to the side, scored a try and converted it as he continued to show the form that others around him were not. The referee came in for some criticism, not just from the visitors, but also the crowd who felt he had spoiled the game as a spectacle. Perhaps the tourists' complaints were not as unjustified as people and the press thought?

The Saturday match found the tourists in Nelson to play a Nelson and Marlborough select. It was a better performance, but against a side not considered to be that strong. Jackson, who had retained his place, kicked a goal in a 12–0 victory for the visitors. Pundits at the game felt Jackson was not only the best forward on the field, but also had played his best game on the tour to date.

He was showing the sort of form that had got him selected in the first place and producing it consistently. It also showed how quickly he had adapted to the New Zealand 'mentality' of winning as the first and only objective of the game, although he would have experienced this when playing in the Northern Union for Swinton. It would prove to be the last time he would pull on the red-and-white banded shirt of the Anglo-Welsh on the tour.

The *Nelson Evening Mail*'s report on the match quoted from an article in the *Athletic News* back home by 'The Bard' of Jackson's play: "English critics are of the opinion that F. Jackson who so ably leads the Leicester and Cornwall forwards is a certainty for an England international cap next season"

It is hard to understand just how he could come to that conclusion given the furore surrounding Jackson in the press back home. The only explanation is that the article must have been written before the RFU AGM and sent to New Zealand via the mail boat.

As events were reaching a critical stage back home in London Jackson was busy preparing for the second test match against the All Blacks. The team had been selected, although as was the tourists' practice it had not been released to the press. As the week progressed the training intensified because everyone knew the whole tour rested on this second encounter with the All Blacks. A win and the tour would be back on track, defeat and the tour was going to be a long hard slog with no reward. The players were training hard, stung by the criticism they had received from the press and unhappy with the way referees were ruling in the matches.

The tour manager, Mr Harnett, had consequently arranged a meeting with the New Zealand union officials and the test referee about how the laws were being interpreted in the hope of clarifying how the referee would rule on certain aspects of play. For some time the tourists had felt that they were suffering from the inconsistencies of referees, coupled with the differing interpretation of the rules by the host officials. However, that meeting would become the least of Harnett's worries for on 23 June the RFU committee were meeting and high on the agenda was the ongoing Jackson saga.

At that meeting the full RFU committee heard a report from the professional sub-committee into the numerous allegations it had received with regard to Fred Jackson who was in New Zealand with the tour party. The furore in the media about the case was not subsiding and they also were watching what the RFU would do carefully. The implication was that they knew more than they had printed but were keeping their powder dry awaiting the rugby union decision. The sub-committee, having examined all the claims and allegations, believed that Jackson of Leicester and Jones, the Swinton professional, were one and the same player. They also thought that Jackson/Jones was really Gabe, a Welshman. They reported the same to the full committee of the rugby union. After hearing the report there was a short discussion by the full committee on the matter and a decision was reached.

The minutes of that meeting said: "Jackson Case. Proposed by Baxter and seconded by Stanley that Jackson be suspended by cable, pending his giving satisfactory proof of not having infringed the laws as to professionalism and that he return home forthwith. Carried."

The following cable was then sent: 'Jackson suspended return him forthwith'.

There is no doubt that this was a major blow to the leadership of the RFU and to the selectors of the Anglo-Welsh tour party. They had selected a player who was now suspected of having played as a professional as far back as the 1901–02 season. The other problem was that it seemed many people and club officials were aware of his history and had chosen for whatever reason to keep quiet about the matter. It may well have been a case of 'people in glass houses should not throw stones', but Jackson's past seems to have been something of an open secret to all except the RFU's professionalism sub-committee and other officials, or perhaps not! Perhaps even they knew but felt it was better to let sleeping dogs lie rather than stir up the sort of publicity they were now having to deal with?

There is little doubt that the RFU was between a rock and a hard place. Clubs and officials had come forward and admitted that they had played against Jackson, knowing full well that he was also Gabe. That admission in itself did not place them in breach of the professionalism laws. However, when clubs also admitted that they had played against Jackson knowing he was Jones, the former Swinton NU player was a different matter. That admission was enough for the RFU to throw them out of the game for being 'professionalised' by having knowingly played against a professional player. It is inconceivable that the clubs would have placed themselves in such a position; therefore it can only be assumed that there was in effect an amnesty for such clubs from the sub-committee or the RFU so that they could gather evidence against Jackson.

Given the high profile Jackson had in the recent past there was little doubt that the newspapers would have a field day once the story was released as it would have to be. In New Zealand the tour manager, Mr Harding, and the players were also in for a dreadful shock. And how would Jackson receive the news, with a sense of shock or would it be relief? It was not going to be long before the whole sorry story was in the public domain. However, Jackson continued with his deception even in the face of overwhelming evidence as to his 'crime'. He told both his colleagues and the tour management that he had no idea why he was being called back to London. Maybe he really didn't have any idea, felt that all the allegations were behind him and some other charge was being laid against him. But it is more likely that he knew full well that his past had caught up with him. Only he could answer such a question.

47

Jackson starts a dribbling rush.
Cartoon published in the *Otago Witness* 10 June 1908
(Picture courtesy of the Alexander Turnbull Library, Wellington, New Zealand)

7. Cut adrift by Leicester

With the cable sent, Jackson's fate in rugby union was effectively sealed unless he was to return home and defend himself against the charges. Now it was a case of damage limitation by all those involved with the affair. The professional sub-committee claimed that they had carried out their remit and recommended that Jackson be suspended until such time that he returned home to England to answer and refute the charges that he was a professional having played for Swinton under the name of John Jones. They would have claimed that the new evidence they had received was more conclusive than that previously offered against Jackson. How it could be more conclusive than a legally sworn affidavit from Swinton is hard to understand. The RFU followed the same line, claiming that their officials had acted swiftly and decisively once unambiguous clear evidence was placed before the sub-committee. What they did not do was disclose just how they had managed to obtain such clear evidence against Jackson when they had been unable to do so prior to the AGM. They would not admit that they had turned a blind eye to those clubs providing evidence to them that incriminated the clubs themselves. It was Leicester that was under the spotlight once the story hit the newspapers.

On the club's behalf, Tom Crumbie, tried to take the moral high ground when the story became public. On 26 June 1908 the *Daily Chronicle* report included a paragraph which can be attributed to Crumbie: "On behalf of the Leicester club it is urged that they acted in good faith on the strength of him (Jackson) having played for Cornwall County and Plymouth, and that he was only an on-off player for the Leicester club for four seasons. The Leicester club now not unreasonably declare that if other clubs and officials had the information that Jackson was another name for Gabe they ought in fairness to have pointed this out to the Leicester club. By playing against Gabe in the name of Jackson these clubs were breaking the rules with full knowledge, whereas Leicester where absolutely in the dark and in complete ignorance of the actual state of affairs."

Crumbie deliberately missed the key point – the real problem was not if Jackson was Gabe, but rather was Jackson really Jones and did Crumbie actually know that? The other key point he forgot to mention to the reporter was that in 1906 he had put forward Jackson's name for selection by the Midland Counties Union, only to withdraw it on advice from the County officials. At that time he had admitted to knowing full well that Jackson was really Gabe, therefore he had known of the Gabe connection for at least two years and possible more.

Ironically, there was a Moseley player who had been playing under an alias. One of their players, Doctor Baxter, on achieving his medical degree had then played for the club using an alias, thus separating his sporting life from his professional life.

Crumbie also failed to mention that Jackson, as Gabe, had been referred to the professional sub-committee accused of being Jones the Swinton professional. As club secretary this is some thing he must have been fully aware of in December 1906. Now he was placing responsibility for all the adverse publicity firmly onto the clubs that Leicester had played against. The inference made by Crumbie was that Leicester had no idea what Jackson was up to and they were totally innocent in the whole affair.

To reinforce this he even had the audacity to say that the foremost forward in English rugby was nothing more than an 'off-and-on player'. Jackson was the club's top scorer at the time, someone who had helped Cornwall to the County Championship and was taking New Zealand by storm with his play. If Crumbie thought his statement was going to deflect criticism from the club he was sadly mistaken.

As news of the Jackson saga spread and other articles appeared in newspapers more and more people came out of the woodwork to say what they knew, or supposedly knew, about Jackson's dubious status. Certainly the newspapers had a field day covering the controversy. They also wanted to know how many clubs had turned a blind eye to Jackson and why they had done so. This was an area the RFU seemed reluctant to delve into for fear of what they might uncover.

While all of this was happening back home, the first that Jackson knew of all this was when the tour manager, Mr Harnett, and the captain Harding summoned him to a meeting on the Wednesday that the cable arrived. Harnett, for his part, would have been mystified on receiving the short cablegram; after all it told him nothing. There was no reason given for the suspension. The skipper, Harding would also have been equally puzzled. The problem they faced was simply what to do about it. Obviously they would need to talk to Jackson, but just what about, they had no idea. There was little they could actually tell him other than what was in the cablegram, namely 'Jackson suspended return him forthwith.'

Harnett did as ordered and reported to the New Zealand press that Jackson had been suspended by his home union and consequently would play no further part in the tour to New Zealand and Australia. He also informed the press that arrangement had been made with the New Zealand Rugby Union for Jackson to be sent home as soon as possible. It was reported that Harding was distraught at losing not only a good friend, but probably the best forward in the tour party and all this just a few days before the vital second test match. The New Zealand press were somewhat perplexed by the decision and were quick to say so, they felt that the whole affair would be better handled had the RFU simply let the tour run its course and then confronted Jackson on his return to London.

It was a course of action that the RFU simply could not follow, to do so would have led to them facing ridicule in England given the attitude of the press and some of their own county unions and individuals. On Thursday 26 June, most of the tour party accompanied Jackson to the dockside in Wellington where he was to board the steamer Maitai to sail off on the four day trip to Sydney. It was a very emotional affair because many of the players were genuinely upset at the manner of Jackson's treatment. They also were aware that they were losing the one forward who had proved to be more than a match for the New Zealanders they had faced.

Jackson sailed away on the first leg of his journey across the Tasman Sea to Sydney. There he was supposed to board a ship to return him to London. Once home he would then face the Rugby Union committee to answer the allegations that he was John. R. Jones the Swinton professional.

Not for the first time, Jackson was about to do what no one expected. Before he boarded ship he was interviewed by a number of reporters, to whom he continued to proclaim both his innocence and stated he had no knowledge of why he had been recalled. The *Otago Witness* reporter said on 1 July: "In an interview Mr F. Jackson expressed himself very pleased with the kindness and hospitality which he and the members of the team had received in New Zealand. He stated that they had particularly enjoyed their trip to the West Coast through the Otira Gorge. On the subject of his disqualification, he preferred to say nothing at present. There was, he said, no compulsion on him to return at once, but in the interests of the team he had decided to acquiesce in the decision that had been arrived at. When he reached England he would have something to say."

Jackson says nothing in the interview really, but did point out that there was no reason why he should return home to England. The article went on to say that the tour captain and manager had no idea what circumstances had led up to Jackson being disqualified. The reporter once again said that the home union would perhaps have been better served to have delayed the decision until the close of the tour and then they could have fully investigated whatever charges were made against the player. Jackson's closing words were: "that he had no knowledge whatever of the exact nature of those charges."

Somewhat prophetically, the reporters own 'last words' in the article were that 'Jackson may eventually settle in Sydney.

In another piece in the *Otago Witness* of the same day, Jackson seems to have given out another apparent red herring as it were, for that reporter wrote: "F. Jackson, the Anglo-Welsh footballer who has been suspended by the English Rugby Union on a charge of professionalism, served all through the South African War which he entered as a private and finished with a commission."

It seems inconceivable that Jackson would not have put such information into his 'pen-picture' at the start of the tour. Now, on leaving New Zealand, he made the claim about his military service when there is no chance it could be questioned. In fairness though it is the same claim he made to the Manchester reporter seven years earlier. He was, in fact, telling the truth. The other interesting point is that it is now known what the charge was against Jackson, professionalism. That information could only have come from London via cablegram, yet the tour management still maintained they were ignorant of the charges laid against him.

All kinds of speculation and rumour were flying around at this time about Jackson and his future. One writer in *The Star* in New Zealand expressed a view that many rugby supporters in the Dominion also held when he wrote: "I notice the cablegram states that Jackson is to return home, but I doubt if the English Union has power to dictate to a player in that manner".

Just a couple of weeks after Jackson set sail for Sydney, the *New Zealand Truth* newspaper writer who produced a gossip column called 'Outside Chat' wrote a piece on the suspension that puts a totally new slant on proceedings and also opened up a whole new can of worms about professionalism and Jackson. On 11 July 1908 he wrote: "A question of the acceptance of a £50 fee to do some recruiting work for the Northern Union people, is alleged to be the real reason for the recall of Jackson by the English Rugby Union. If the Cornwall man is up to snuff he will flatten out the old fossils who boss bastard rugby in the Old Dart in one act that is if the circumstances as reported to me are correct. But why make fish of one and flesh of another? If Jackson is culpable, so is another member of the party now round these parts and in a much greater degree. He has cunningly cloaked up his real intentions so as to hoodwink the derelicts who, barnacle-like have attached themselves to the sinking rugby union ship in Fogland. The writer is in possession of certain information from a friend in London regarding several little matters which would give manager Harnett a shock where it recorded in cold type…"

There are a number of issues raised by the article, not least the suggestion that Jackson had been paid £50 by the Northern Union to scout for talent for the new code. It is not clear who the writer suggests paid this £50 to Jackson. It is difficult to see how the Northern Union could have any contact with him without letting Swinton know, although he could have been acting on behalf of a particular club. Maybe the writer was mistaking the £50 fee for a signing on fee that Swinton gave to Jackson back in 1901, but that was seven years earlier. Maybe the fledgling New Zealand Northern Union people approached him, but why should they?

It is the second implication in the piece which is much nearer the mark; that one other member of the tour party was in fact a professional and that was seemingly an open secret. This allegation was subsequently proved to be correct. The article would have offered Jackson little comfort, but did highlight the fact that he was not the only guilty one under the RFU's rules.

Jackson seems to have thwarted the authorities over his status throughout his playing career, and he was not about to succumb now. He may have been ordered home, but that did not mean he would go home. He had in his pocket a ticket to sail to England. If he chose not to use it then it would afford him some financial collateral. He knew full well that if he ever set foot on English soil the rugby officials of both codes would be after him to answer charges that he was a professional, or in breach of contract as a professional, as the case may be. That may not have bothered him; no doubt he would simply have continued to deny the allegations. He had covered his tracks throughout his playing career by the clever use of aliases.

On the other hand, he would have known that Swinton would be waiting for him once he arrived in the country. They would be a different proposition because they had made it known that on his return they intended to take legal action against him. It was their contention that Jackson was Jones and he had signed for the club for a fee of £40. Having walked out on the club he was in breach of contract. In those days when a player signed for a Northern Union club he was there 'for life', which meant in essence the club owned the playing rights of the player for as long as they wanted.

Jackson knew that in a court of law he would be faced with having to tell the truth or risk perjury, a very serious offence. It could well have been that other secrets may have been let out of the bag in a court case. For example, just who was he? Where had he been educated, had he stolen other people's identities and if so why? The consequences of such information coming out would not have been what he wanted. He had always avoided placing himself in a position where he was forced to divulge anything about himself which he did not want to.

Whatever the reasons, Jackson set off to return to England but he never arrived. As the Maitai sailed out of Wellington his team mates stood on the dockside, many in tears as they waved their colleague off. Little did they know at that time that he probably had no intention of returning home, but was to return to the country he would make his new home, New Zealand. They also were unaware that there was a very important reason why he would want to return to New Zealand rather than England; it was to protect his true identity.

8. Jackson or Gabe?

Jackson would have stood on deck and looked down on his fellow players knowing that all he possessed was probably in his berth below decks. It is not clear how much money, if any, he had in is possession or how he was going to live, but one thing was probably clear in his mind, travelling home was not an option. He had no intention of having to go into a court of law to defend himself. Travelling to Australia would have caused him few, if any problems; after all he had travelled as a teenager to South Africa and survived in that country.

There was a problem in Australia that he probably knew little about, which would have caused him to worry if he was in need of cash, or wanted to earn cash. After the 1907–08 Northern Union tour that Albert Baskerville had organised, the New Zealand NU tourists stopped off in Sydney to play a three match series against the newly formed New South Wales Rugby League. The funds raised by that series had been sufficient to allow the fledgling Northern Union code to set up their own professional rugby league and in 1908 the first ever rugby league season had got under way.

The knock-on effect from that was a rugby war was raging in Sydney between the new league and the old union which was under the control of the Metropolitan Rugby Union. The war was in many ways similar to that which had been waged in England in 1895, the remnants of which were still going on as Jackson would have found to his cost. The union code had control of most of the enclosed grounds in the city and thought that this would give them a stranglehold to kill the new league before it even got going. If the new league was to survive, it needed to play its games on enclosed grounds to allow them to collect gate money That had not proved to be the case as a number of grounds and their management felt the rugby union was being very unfair in its treatment of the new league and had given the new league the go ahead to rent their grounds, much to the anger of the rugby union officials. On 30 June, when Jackson landed at Sydney, he would have probably found few, if any, friends in either code.

The first ever season of professional rugby league had kicked off on Easter Monday 1908. A New Zealand Maori team had begun a tour under the Northern Union code, so there was plenty of league activity and there may have been no need for Jackson's talents at such a late stage in the season.

In rugby union, the Metropolitan Rugby Union was supportive of the RFU in every possible way. Sometimes the clubs and players felt that they were more concerned with pleasing the English Union than looking after the interests of the Australian game and its players.

The Australian union had agreed to send a team to tour England and Wales at the end of the season. One reason for this was the hope that it would stop players from switching to rugby league. The lure of a tour to the 'Old Country', it was felt, would stop the top players from defecting. That being the case, they would not want to be associated with Jackson and the taint of professionalism that came with him.

News of Jackson's suspension by the RFU would have followed him across the Tasman Sea, so he would have found no support in Sydney from the union fraternity. If he thought he could continue to bluff his way out of his predicament, then an article published on 30 June in *The Daily Chronicle* in England would have quickly dispelled such thoughts. As was said earlier, once Jackson's fate had moved into the public domain, many people who previously had sat back took the opportunity of jumping on the band wagon.

For the first time a direct link between Jackson and the Jones of Swinton became public. The article said: "...The case is also exciting great interest in Northern Rugby football circles by reason of Jackson's association with Swinton under the name John Jones. Evidence has come in from all quarters that Jackson and John Jones are undoubtedly Gabe the well-known forward of the famous Swansea club."

The article is the second reference to Jackson being Gabe, the first was in the *Cardiff Evening Express* and this suggests that his true identity was Gabe and that he was born of Welsh parents in Morriston. However, the reference made in the Cardiff newspaper could not be found; maybe the wrong newspaper was quoted in the Leicester club history. The second problem is that 'the famous Swansea club' has no record of a 'Gabe' playing for them during the period Jackson is supposed to have played. However, at the turn of the century, Morriston had a very strong rugby union club which played regularly against leading clubs in Wales, including Neath, Cardiff and Llanelli. Perhaps Morriston was indeed the 'famous Swansea club'.

There was a Gabe family reported to be living in Morriston in 1891; however of the two sons that could well have been Jackson because they were born within a reasonable time frame, neither stands up to scrutiny. Both of the Gabes were shown on the 1911 census as still living in Glamorgan and at that time Jackson was in New Zealand. There is another explanation, namely that the press having picked up on the name Gabe assumed it to be his true identity. Maybe it was simply another of his aliases, given that a Rhys Gabe was still playing at the time in Cardiff.

It is, however, inconceivable that so many people would come forward and claim that Jackson was really Gabe if he was not. Also, many players said that they had actually played against him when he was at Swansea. Recent investigations have shown that there is no record of a Gabe playing for the two other clubs in the Swansea area, namely Neath and Llanelli. The local newspapers had limited coverage of the Morriston club, so proving that Jackson played there is difficult. It is as if Gabe, the goalkicking forward, never existed; nothing new there then!

The article in the *Daily Chronicle* from the time the story first broke went on to pose a vital question for the rugby union followers and the answer was not complimentary to the game. The article said: "The crucial point in which attention is now being directed is whether it can be demonstrated that a number of clubs in the RU were aware that Jackson was the same person who played under the name of John Jones for Swinton as a NU player. That is the point which the Leicester club, its members and supporters desire to have cleared up."

It would appear that Crumbie's actions in attempting to gain the high moral ground in this matter had been successful. The *Chronicle* had seemingly followed his lead that the club knew nothing about the whole Jackson affair and if others did they had a duty to inform the club. The article continued to answer the question it had posed: "It is now admitted by a number of clubs that they did have this knowledge, and it was their duty as members of the RU to communicate that knowledge to the club and county most vitally interested in order that they might avoid as far as possible any breach of the laws. It would not matter that Gabe, of Swansea, afterwards played in the assumed name of Jackson, because that is frequently done for private reasons."

So, according to the *Chronicle*, clubs knew full well that Jackson was Gabe, which was not so bad, but they also knew that Jackson or Gabe was the John Jones that had played for Swinton. While Jackson had been hung out to dry by the RFU without the benefit of being able to submit a defence, it seems that the clubs suffered no such retribution. Yet, by their own laws, any player playing against a professional would automatically professionalise themselves. Any club which had condoned playing against Jackson knowing him to be Jones had also breached the professionalism laws. Now club officials were coming forward and claiming quite openly that they knew of Jackson's history and yet they had still allowed matches to go ahead contrary to the rugby union rules about professionalism in force at that time.

There is evidence that even the rugby union authorities knew full well just what the situation was with Jackson and his professional past. On 25 August 1908, in New Zealand, the *Poverty Bay Herald* published an article it had 'cribbed, from the *Standard* in England. In that article that was headlined "Jackson Alias Gabe" they quoted the English report, saying: "Jackson is an old Swansea player named Ivor Gabe who has played with Swinton, members of the Northern Union and the facts seem to have been pretty generally known when he was selected as one of the British team... Jackson is not Jackson at all but an old professional who has been with many clubs."

This would support the view that the authorities were fully aware of Jackson's status, but chose, for whatever reasons, to take no action. Perhaps they acted on the advice of the professional sub-committee who could find no evidence to convict Jackson. It would also explain why, even when Jackson was playing very well, he was not selected for the England team. It also seems that now they had the evidence against him obtained by whatever means they were going to extract full revenge for the problems he had caused them, even if they did not take action against the clubs and people providing the evidence.

Rhys Gabe.

58

No club was to suffer any recriminations and in January 1909 as shall become clear, even Leicester, who were at the very centre of the controversy and who eventually had four of their players declared to be 'professional', were deemed to be not guilty of breaking the laws of the game. It appeared that the RFU was very reluctant to take action against clubs in general – and Leicester in particular – who admitted to knowing Jackson was Jones. The key reason was the risk of that club joining their arch rivals, the Northern Union, if they were banned by the RFU. And if one major club, in particular Leicester, had joined the NU, the knock on effect of lost fixtures, especially with local rivals, could have driven other clubs to sign up with the Northern Union. As had happened in the north of England after 1895, the RFU could have been reduced to a rump in key areas of the country, especially the east midlands. The RFU took the easy option of simply punishing Jackson while they let the clubs get off scot free. But with the future of their union at stake, did they have any choice?

Having read the first half of the article in the *Daily Chronicle*, Crumbie, the Leicester club, its members and supporters would have felt that they and the club were home and dry and the moral high ground was theirs. However, the *Chronicle* did raise another issue in the article. The newspaper claimed that they had received a lot of correspondence on the matter, but they chose to print only one letter. It was from Perry Adams of the Old Edwardians club in Birmingham. This was the same Adams who had seconded the Moseley motion at the RFU AGM at the end of May. He was also a member of the Midlands Counties Union committee, so he was not exactly neutral. In his letter he laid bare the suggestion that Tom Crumbie was as blameless and in the dark on the whole affair as he claimed: "Sir – the story... about the mystery that surrounds the 'Jackson case' prompts me to place a few facts before you.

Mr T. Crumbie, the honorary sec of Leicester FC, proposed 'Jackson' for a place in the Midland Counties team some years ago, but withdrew his name as he was told that the MCFU did not wish Jackson to represent them. Mr Crumbie then acknowledged that his name was Gabe. Mr Gil Evans the well-known referee, remembered him at school as Gabe.

It is very comic of Mr Crumbie now to adopt the righteous indignant attitude of injured innocence. Suspicion has hung about this player for years, and it was never made public what induced him, first of all, to leave Cornwall for Plymouth and afterwards to leave Plymouth for Leicester. His name and story were given to the Professional Sub

Committee in December 1906 as a definite case for their inquiry. That committee were told that if they would produce a photograph of him, which it was impossible to get, positive proof of his professionalism could be obtained. This offer the sub-committee treated with contempt and negligence. The selectors of the British team, shortly after this, with full knowledge of the suspicion and charges against 'Jackson' included him in the team for New Zealand. It was left for a private individual to obtain a photograph of Jackson as it appeared in the group of the Cornwall team, taken at the final match of the County Championship this year. Then the absolute proof against 'Jackson' was obtained and produced at the RFU general meeting on May 28."

Crumbie's economical use of the truth had been exposed and, more importantly, so had the RFU. The proof of Jackson's professional past had been given at the AGM, but the Moseley motion was still lost. Given Adams's position within the Midland Counties Union it is highly likely that he would have been involved in 1906 in deciding that Jackson was not wanted by the Midland Counties team because of the baggage he brought with him. The Moseley club would see their action in proposing the motion at the AGM as fully justified by the newspaper's revelations. The other point to note is that the article tends to support the notion mentioned earlier that someone had taken it upon themselves to make sure that the photograph in question found its way into the hands of the Swinton club. Maybe it was Adams himself who ensured the photograph of Jackson was sent to Swinton. There seems to have been a concerted effort to pin down Jackson.

There is one other important fact contained in Adams letter and that is the comment about Gil Evans the referee. Evans had been a player for Swansea in the 1890s and had captained the second team during the 1895–96 season. The other important information is that Evans was a school teacher and reportedly worked in Swansea in 1898 before moving to the Midlands. Evans, it is implied by Adams, remembered Jackson at school where he was called Gabe. This would support the view that Jackson was a Morriston man who had been educated in the Swansea area and possibly taught by Evans. This would also fit in with the newspaper quote in the 1994 history of the Leicester club that "Jackson was a Cymro". After all this time there is little chance of identifying which schools Evans taught at and even less chance that the admissions registers for those schools still exist.

It was no surprise that Jackson took the opportunity of staying in Australia until the dust settled on the whole affair. He would not however, as he had intimated to the New Zealand press, settle in Sydney. As shall become clear, his heart lay in another country.

Jackson began making plans that would see him sail away from Sydney. How he survived for 12 weeks in Australia will probably never be known. Did he play on his reputation as an international rugby player to get sympathisers to offer him accommodation during his time in Australia? Did Northern Union officials woo him in an attempt to get him to turn to their game? Both are possible but his future was to be back in New Zealand.

There is a very sad postscript to the ill-fated tour concerning the tour manager, George Harnett. *The New Zealand Truth* on 15 July 1911 carried a story which read: "The annual meeting of the English Rugby Union held some slight interest for New Zealanders, owing to the fact that thee was an organised attempt, successful as it turned out, to deprive George H. Hartnett of his acknowledged right to become junior vice president of that august body. Geo. H. will be remembered here as manager of the Anglo-Welsh team that last toured this Dominion and, on this occasion, was obliged to put up with defeat by 180 to 157 votes – one Prescott beating him. Evidently George is not the only pebble on the beach in Rugby circles in his own country, although a lot of foolish people out here thought he was, or very near it. At least, he made them think so."

It would seem that the RFU's leading officials had not forgotten or forgiven Harnett for the ills and bad publicity that had befallen that tour and the professionalism fiasco that followed it. They had exacted revenge on Jackson, but were not satisfied with that and were going to exact similar retribution against the manager of that tour also. Harnett died in 1930. He was still active for the Wasps club, but was probably saddened by the attitude towards him by some within the RFU.

George Hartnett

9. Return to New Zealand

Toward the end of his 12 weeks in Australia, Jackson, or perhaps more accurately, a friend of his, wrote to the treasurer of the New Zealand Rugby Union with a proposition. Reading between the lines it seems that back in June his passage home from New Zealand to London had been funded by the New Zealand union. Jackson had not used his ticket home to London and now wanted to use it as collateral in a deal with the NZRU. He proposed to return the ticket to the union in return for a ticket back to Wellington. Given that a single ticket to London in 1908 would have cost around £40 and a ticket to New Zealand around £3, it would have been good business to agree to his suggestion. Ron Palenski in *All-Blacks v Lions* wrote of the approach by an unknown person: "have seen Jackson and it appears he wants to return to New Zealand' the letter said. 'He offered to hand over his ticket to London in consideration of a ticket to Wellington.' A deal was struck; Jackson cancelled his homeward passage and boarded a ship for Wellington."

Jackson may have wanted a little cash as well to go some way to making up the shortfall. If he only received £20 or so it would be more than enough to sustain him in New Zealand for some time if used prudently. The other fact that supports such an idea is that the NZRU treasurer Mr Galbraith had been assigned to travel around the country with the Anglo-Welsh tourists, and acted as a general factotum. It is not unreasonable to assume that he would have had a good deal of contact with Jackson on his travels.

There is no doubt that the NZRU officials had some sympathy for Jackson. They had little knowledge of the background to his suspension. They were aware that in England a player seen talking to an NU player or an NU club official could and would be deemed to be 'professionalised' them by the RFU officials. To the New Zealanders that went against their view of natural justice. In a more pragmatic way, they could see that the tour was failing financially because of the attitude of the touring players. Further evidence of this was supplied by R.A. Barr after the tour in his book *British Rugby Team in Maoriland – True Story of the Tour*. He told many stories of off-field activities and referred too many of the tourists "falling for young ladies and vice versa". Now their star forward had been recalled. From the point of view of making the tour a success, it would have been prudent to sit on matters until the tour was over and the players were back home. Then an investigation could have been carried out without disrupting the tour. It is not unreasonable to assume that the New Zealand RU officials would agree to Jackson's suggestion and collude with him at the expense of the English union.

On Sunday 14 September Jackson returned to the dockside in Sydney. There he re-boarded the Maitai, which was bound for Wellington. Given his prowess on the rugby field and the fact that professional NU rugby barely existed in New Zealand at that time, but did in Australia, it seems odd he chose to return to New Zealand. Maybe playing NU rugby did not interest him enough to remain in Australia. It seems that Jackson was burning his boats with his old life and setting out to start afresh in a new country. Even at the outset of this new beginning he could not help courting controversy, although this time perhaps for all the right reasons.

When the Maitai docked Jackson disembarked and quickly found himself in trouble, but not involving football. Soon after setting foot on New Zealand soil he was arrested. An article about Jackson appeared in the *Nelson Evening Mail* on 18 September 1908: "...Nothing was heard of him until he made rather a noteworthy return to Wellington yesterday, having come back from Sydney again on the steamer Maitai. At present there is considerable doubt as to the real facts of the case, but it has been gathered that on the trip over from Sydney trouble arose amongst the passengers. A man named William Lewis is alleged to have obtained from a young fellow passenger a sum of £15 by means of some card game, and the young man being of the opinion that he had been swindled complained to his fellow passengers. When the vessel reached Wellington, the sum of £5 was returned to the young man by Lewis, who, it is said, had an idea he was likely to get into trouble over the affair.

After the passengers had come ashore, Jackson met Lewis in front of the post office and, it is alleged, with a view to seeing justice done to the young man, grabbed Lewis by the vest, and demanded that he should refund the remaining £10. Sergeant Dale and Constable Fleming, who were in the vicinity, came up and asked the two men to go along to the police station. They did so and there Lewis had a warrant issued for Jackson's arrest on a charge of assault. The warrant was executed, and Jackson was immediately brought before Dr. A McArthur, S.M., and charged with the offence alleged against him. He was remanded until this morning and in the meantime was allowed his freedom, having laid down a cash deposit of £5 as a bond for his appearance before the Magistrate today."

Why would Jackson court such publicity? To do so was not his style. For the first time there is an insight into what made him tick. He was not prepared to let a young man be swindled out of what was a considerable sum of money in 1908 and was also prepared to do something about it. The other interesting point is that he was obviously not without funds because he handed over a £5 bond to cover his bail. From the resulting trial, it became clear that he had travelled over on the Maitai saloon class, not 'steerage' so had money to travel in comfort. Either he had been working in Sydney, or maybe he had obtained some funds from the NZRU.

It was only on the following day, Friday 19 September that the full story unfolded in court and then only because Jackson's solicitor insisted that it be told. Jackson had attracted a lot of interest from the press and the allegation of assault would not have sat well for him had it been proved. Probably both the solicitor and Jackson were well aware of the old maxim 'if you throw mud some of it will stick'. Both were determined to ensure that Jackson's record was unblemished when he walked away from the Magistrates Court that morning.

The *Otago Witness* gave a full account of events that took place in the court on 23 September 1908. It would seem the cheating at cards by Lewis was only the tip of the iceberg when it came to the unfortunate young man who had lost the large sum of money. The article was headed: "Charge against Jackson dismissed". It said: "There was a tremor of excitement in the Wellington Police Court on Friday when the name of Frederick Jackson, of the British Rugby team, was called. Jackson stepped briskly from the back of the court with a nod to a detective, and took up his stand in the dock with a broad smile. He was charged with having assaulted William Lewis, and through Mr Wilford, who appeared on his behalf, pleaded 'Not guilty'.

The informant, William Lewis, was placed in the box. When told to state the facts to his Worship, he said: 'When I went to the Police Station I did not have time to speak to anyone who saw the assault, and when I came back there was no one there. I have no witnesses, and don't wish to go on with the case.'

Mr Wilford: 'I have something to say, you're Worship.'

His Worship: 'I don't think it's necessary, Mr Wilford.'

Mr Wilford: 'Yes, it is, your Worship, in the interests of my client. A great deal of publicity has been given to this case, and I must say something about it.'

His Worship having given his permission, Mr Wilford detailed what he said were the facts of the case. The defendant had been a saloon passenger on the Maitai, whilst the complainant had been travelling steerage. Lewis went on board with a companion, neither paying their

65

fares. The stewards managed to get Lewis's fare from him, but the police boat had to come off and take his companion from the ship. On the boat was another passenger, a young man, who recognised Lewis as the man who had played a confidence trick on him some days before. Lewis had met the young man and asked him if he was going to New Zealand, as he had some dogs to take over to Christchurch. He asked the young man to help him, and if he did so he would give him a billet on his farm at Christchurch. The young man agreed, and was then taken by Lewis to the offices of the Melbourne Shipping Company. Here Lewis said he was £2 short of the amount needed for some business he had to do, and asked for a loan of that amount. The Young man, who, Mr. Wilford said, was obviously from the back-blocks, took out his purse, which contained £14, to take out the £2, and Lewis snatched the purse and disappeared through the office. The young man lost sight of him, and never saw him again until he met him on the Maitai. On the trip over Lewis met a young Scotsman named Chisholm, off whom he won £4 by means of a card game known as 'farmers' glory'. He then got a 'cold deck' on Chisholm at poker. When the vessel reached Wellington, Detective Lewis came on board. A complaint was made to Detective Lewis who spoke to the complainant Lewis. The complainant Lewis handed over to the young man the sum of £5. What had become of the other £9 Mr. Wilford could not say, but Lewis could not have had the whole of it, as he had used part of it to pay his fare. When the passengers came ashore at Wellington the young man and Chisholm told Jackson about what had happened. Jackson subsequently met Lewis whom he described as a white-livered cur, and catching Lewis by the vest demanded that the money should be handed over to the young man. 'What Jackson ought to get', said Mr Wilford, 'is a testimonial.'

If the case had gone on with, the defence would have been that that the complainant was a spieler.

Lewis: 'I beg your pardon. You can't prove that. There is not a conviction against me in New Zealand.'

His Worship: 'There is no need to go any further, Mr. Wilford.'

The case was struck out."

His solicitor, Mr Wilford, was a well known Wellington rugby enthusiast and would later become a Liberal Member of Parliament and went on to become leader of the Liberal Party in New Zealand. Perhaps he offered his services as a favour to Jackson whom he would undoubtedly have heard of and in all probability admired.

10. Travels around New Zealand

So Jackson left the court with his reputation intact. It was a case that did show the measure of Jackson; here was a man who wanted to return quietly to New Zealand. Yet he was prepared to risk losing that anonymity by getting into trouble with the law simply to help a young man whom he did not even know. It suggests that Jackson had a strong sense of what was right and wrong. Believing that the young man was not in a position to right the wrong done to him, Jackson took it upon himself to seek retribution for him.

As well as paying for his trip and his bail, Jackson was able to hire a solicitor to represent him in court and that would have cost him money.

When he left the court he began his travels through the country and while there is evidence of his travelling, there is no evidence of how he earned his living. He also tried to keep all his rugby options open by trying to keep the rugby union side of things happy while at the same time courting the fledgling Northern Union code in the country as a possible source of income.

Back in England the RFU continued to await his return and if Tom Crumbie thought his and Leicester's troubles were over he was wrong. Moseley, along with the Midland Counties Union had won the case against Jackson, but they considered it a victory in battle rather than a victory in the war. They had a bigger target in their sights, namely the Leicester club itself.

Their contention was that Leicester had knowingly played Jackson and others while fully aware of their professional status, and that the club were guilty of offering illegal inducements to players to join their club. If that were the case then the club was as guilty as the players and should therefore be thrown out of the RFU for professionalism. Suddenly the problems caused by Fred Jackson paled into insignificance as a major club in the sport was threatened with expulsion. Leicester were coming under increasing attack and their cause was not helped when news broke that Tom Smith, a Leicester player and another of the Anglo-Welsh tourists, had been suspended and was also accused of professionalism.

It now becomes a little difficult to keep track of Jackson's movements. It does seem that he had an itinerary of sorts, although whether it had been planned while still in Sydney or perhaps once he landed in Wellington is not clear. He did intend to travel throughout the South Island, although just how he funded his travels is not known. He could have called on friends he had made on the tour to host him, which they would gladly have done. The first newspaper reference to him comes from the *Otago Witness* of 23 September, just four days after the court encounter.

The article says that he had left Wellington and crossed to Dunedin in the south of the South Island. Also, he was not yet willing to burn his boats with the rugby union code in favour of the fledgling Northern Union. It gives us an idea of his travel plans and finally that he was still keeping up the pretence of his innocence over professionalism. Given the slowness of information travelling from England to New Zealand there was no reason for him not to do so. The article said: "Mr Fred Jackson, one of the best, if not the best, forward in the British Rugby team, who is at present in Dunedin, is not enamoured of the Northern Union game, and opines that it will not prove so attractive as its supporters and admirers think. 'I have seen a lot of Northern Union games,' remarked Jackson to the writer, and the Rugby Union game, if played well, is far ahead of it. What is required in the Rugby Union game is a modification of the rules and intelligence to play it.' There is the matter in a nutshell.

By the way, it has been rumoured that Jackson is out here in the interests of the Northern Unionism. This is furthest from his thoughts; indeed, the big Cornishman's opinion of Northern Union football is not altogether favourable to the code. Jackson's movements at present are undecided. He proposes spending a week or two in Southland, whither he goes in the course of a day or two. By that time he anticipates letters from England, which will make his case of alleged professionalism clear; in fact Jackson is hopeful of being reinstated. It is well to remember that Jackson has only been suspended pending further hearing of his case, and if he is reinstated New Zealand will benefit, for Jackson has stated there is a possibility of his remaining in New Zealand, and more unlikely things might happen than playing under the banner of the New Zealand Rugby Union."

There is more support for the idea that Jackson was involved in some way with the Northern Union code which can be seen from another article, this time in the *Canterbury Times* of 7 October 1908. The report had been sent by the newspaper's Dunedin reporter on 3 October. This was when Jackson had only just returned to New Zealand and was beginning to travel about the country. It read: "F. Jackson, the big Cornish forward of the British team, who was recalled by cable to answer a charge of alleged professionalism, but who returned to New Zealand from Sydney the other day, is at present 'resting' in Dunedin. It is Jackson's intention to go gold-dredging, and with that object he proposes visiting the various gold-dredging centres in the dominion. Jackson is hopeful of being reinstated as an amateur in which case he talks of remaining for some time in New Zealand and playing under the New Zealand Rugby Union's banner. By the way, I cannot see how Jackson can hope for reinstatement when he is only suspended, and must first go to England to 'explain things'. It is rumoured that Jackson is over here in the interests of Northern Unionism, but that is distant from his mind. I had a chat with the big British footballer the other day on the subject, and his opinion of Northern Union football is not flattering to the code."

With regard to his occupation as a mining engineer, this was a pretence that he maintained for some considerable time. After all, it was a New Zealand newspaper that had carried the article in which in a pen picture he had maintained he was such an engineer and educated at Camborne School of Mines. He could scarcely deny it now without throwing doubt on all of the claims he had made about himself. As late as 1911, on the electoral roll for The Bay of Plenty, he is listed as being a mining engineer, something he maintained right up until the 1922 electoral roll. However, in 1913 on his marriage declaration he claims to be 'a contractor', while in 1916 on the census he claims to be 'a fisherman and mail carrier'. From 1925 through to 1942 he claimed is occupation was wharfinger not mining engineer.

The other interesting point from the article is the suggestion that Jackson was travelling through the South Island perhaps at the behest of the Northern Union people in Wellington and Auckland. He always did deny this, but to quote Shakespeare it could well have been a case that the man "Doth protest too much". If there were no truth in the Northern Union angle, why would the newspapers have got hold of the story in the first place and continued to mention it in their articles? That particular idea must have originated somewhere and it could well be that he was in fact acting as an emissary for the new code in the South Island where the new code was not established as strongly as elsewhere in the Dominion.

Unfortunately, all of the early minutes for the Auckland Rugby League were destroyed in a fire many years ago so this cannot be verified. What is known is that another player, George Gillett, who was of a similar standing to Jackson, was employed by the New Zealand Rugby League in 1912 as 'and organiser'. Gillett travelled around the provinces promoting the new code in an attempt to spread its influence to remoter areas. If Jackson had been employed in a similar role back in 1908 or 1909 then surely he would have been paid and had his

69

expenses covered. If that were the case it would go some way to explaining how he financed himself and his travels. However, any idea of letters arriving from England to clear his name was a figment of his imagination. Back in England quite the reverse was happening.

Both Byrne and Adams, who had proposed and seconded the veiled professionalism motion at the AGM back in May, had continued in their quest to rid the game of professionalism and the Leicester club. The information about the allegations against Tom Smith was pounced upon with great glee by the writer in the *New Zealand Truth* in his column in July 1908. Then he had claimed that another member of the tour party was guilty of professionalism. In his column, *General Gossip*, the same reporter wrote on 14 November: "When it was announced that Jackson of the Anglo-Welsh team had been ordered to pack his traps for England at an early stage of the Dominionist tour, presumably to undergo examination in respect to his identity with a well known professional footballer, I made no bones about charging other members of Harding's team with having sailed under false colours as regards their amateur status, but my assertion was scoffed at in certain 'know-all' quarters. The information, however, at my command was quite good enough for me to act upon, and the news which now comes through concerning T. Smith another member of Harding's brigade of rugby failures on a charge of professionalism shows that I was on the right scent after all. And Smith's case is a very mild one compared to that of two other players of the team which buried its reputation deep in Dominion soil...."

If the writer is to be believed then at least four of the tourists were guilty of professionalism before they left for the tour. It would seem that not only Leicester were in murky waters with the RFU and its laws on amateurism, but so were the Anglo-Welsh selectors.

Jackson and Smith were linked with the Leicester captain Matthews who meant that three of the club's players had been barred from the game. Having one player suspended could be bad luck, but three must have meant some form of collusion at the very least and the Leicester officials were thus implicated. It also would appear that all of this was known to everyone except the leadership of the RFU.

In the club's defence, it seems that Matthews had signed a contract with Hull, but received no payment, and never played for the NU club. When he did sign the contract it was not against the union rules; this was only outlawed two years later. The RFU, however, were going to be seen to be ruthless in their pursuit of professionals, but only with 'easy targets'. They dealt retrospectively with Matthews, and suspended him even though he had not broken or transgressed the professionalism rules at the time he signed the contract with Hull.

The RFU committee met on 5 October 1908 to consider the facts and after a lengthy debate, in which no doubt both Byrne and Adams had their say, a decision was reached. The committee decided that Jackson, Smith, Matthews and Hardiman, all from the Leicester club, were professionals and therefore banned from the game. This was despite the fact that Smith and Jackson had not had the chance to offer any sort of defence against the charges. Equally importantly, they also decided that despite previous enquiries into the workings and financial dealings of the Leicester club clearing them of any wrongdoing, the club should be subjected to yet another investigation. It was a decision that caused yet more division within the game and there were fears that a second schism similar to that in 1895 could occur, this time from the midlands rather than the north. Such a split would have proved disastrous for rugby union and could have sounded the death knell for the sport as a national game.

The RFU released their decision to the media in due course and hoped that was the end of the matter. No one thought to send news of that decision down to New Zealand and so the NZRU remained in blissful ignorance of the decision, which suited Jackson. *The Colonist*, a Nelson paper, said on 7 October 1908: "Fred Jackson, the big Cornish forward of the British Rugby team, who has been much in the public eye of late, is still in Dunedin and more unlikely things might happen that he will settle there for some time. It is Jackson's intention to get an insight into the dredging industry in this country, and with that object he purposes to visit the principle gold dredges in Otago. Jackson has a deal of experience as a practical and theoretical miner in Cornwall, but is anxious to gain some knowledge of gold dredging."

By 21 October 1908, just two weeks later, there is another report of his movements in the *Otago Witness.* His actions added further to the idea that he was working for the Northern Union. The article also burst the bubble that he would soon be cleared of the allegations against him back home: "Fred Jackson, the member of the British Rugby team who is at present in New Zealand, has found his way from Dunedin to Wellington, and is working his way to Auckland. By the way, the statement that Jackson proposes remaining in New Zealand until next season in anticipation of having his suspension removed and playing under the banner of the New Zealand Rugby Union is incorrect, in so far as it is impossible for a British footballer to have his suspension removed until he has gone home and defended himself before the

71

English Rugby Union under whose jurisdiction he is. There is I fear little prospect of Jackson playing football in New Zealand."

It was an article which seemed to sound the death knell of his chances of being reinstated into rugby union. Less than a fortnight later, the *Otago Witness* on 4 November carried an article reportedly from England which showed clearly that Jackson's fate back home was settled: "...By the way there is no news of the return of F. Jackson to this country (says a writer in an English newspaper concerning Fred Jackson) I had news of his arrival in Sydney from New Zealand in the middle of July since then he has had plenty of time to reach England and set about his defence, if he deemed that necessary but there is no word of even that.

I have heard that the Swinton club confident that Jackson is their gentleman John Jones have been keeping a watchful eye on the Australian arrivals but have so far been disappointed."

Reading that, Jackson would have known for sure that once he set foot on English soil he would be served with a writ by Swinton who would sue him for breach of contract. Once in court who knows just what Jackson may be faced with and what other skeletons would fall out of his cupboard, for him it was better to stay as far away as possible. Just a month later, in early December, Jackson had left Wellington and, according to the *Nelson Evening Mail,* was visiting Nelson in the South Island. Later developments suggest that he was beginning to put down roots in that area and would, in time, be instrumental in setting up a Northern Union league there.

The New Year brought some sort of closure on the whole affair, in England at least. On 14 and 15 January 1909 the RFU committee met at the Grand Hotel in Leicester. It was their intention to hear all of the evidence the inquiry into the Leicester club had unearthed and listen to the sub-committee's ruling on the matter. A great deal of discussion went on and it was decided that the full committee would deliver their verdict two weeks later.

In essence, the committee then found that the Leicester club was blameless and all charges were dropped. They said that the club had no knowledge that Smith, Jackson, Hardiman and Matthews had played professionally and so could not have taken any action. That seems strange when Jackson had been referred to the professionalism sub-committee back in December 1906. Surely the club would have known this, certainly Tom Crumbie did. Equally strange was the fact that the Leicester club had previously admitted to knowing Matthews has signed a contract for Hull, but he had never played for the club or received any payment. They must also have been aware of the changes made to the rules that made Matthews ineligible to play the game, yet they continued to select him for matches. They could have argued that he had not broken the rules at the time he signed for Hull, and was it fair that the rule change be applied retrospectively?

Finally, it seems incredible that a large number of clubs and players should have known that Jackson was Gabe – and also Jones – yet the Leicester club did not; is it realistic to accept that no one from any other club would have approached Leicester and told them about Jackson's past. That was what the RFU officials decided was the case. There was a further charge involving three other players, and the club was similarly cleared of wrongdoing. Certainly they would have had no knowledge of Smith's decision to sign as a professional while on his way back from the Anglo-Welsh tour.

The RFU committee then poured salt in the wounds of the club's accusers by adding a rider to their decision: "Your committee is strongly of the opinion that the allegations against the Leicester club are largely due to the fact that the club, having a strong team with a good match list, attracts players who are unable to get such good football in other localities but that, however undesirable this may be, the players have not benefited pecuniarily thereby." So everyone was expected to believe that the Leicester club was as 'white as driven snow' over the allegations made against it. More importantly, people were expected to believe that the premier club in the land was being run by the most naive committee in rugby history.

The decision must have been a slap in the face for Byrne and Adams, the Midlands Counties Union and the Moseley club. They must have felt that Leicester had got off scot free, but – with hindsight – it is hard to see just what the RFU officials could have done. To throw the club out of the union would have simply driven it into the waiting arms of the Northern Union who would have welcomed a strong Midlands stronghold. Had that happened there is no way of knowing how many other clubs would have followed Leicester's lead and Northern Union football would have spread from its northern heartland further south to the midlands. Who knows just how far it would have spread after that; certainly the south west and South Wales could have fallen to the NU?

Arnold Crane, the RFU president and a member of the Midland Counties Union, resigned in disgust at the decision to exonerate Leicester. He is the only president to resign from the office. Leicester were in the clear and still operating, as were all those clubs who had admitted playing against Jackson knowing full well he was a classed as a professional. No club or its players suffered any penalties meanwhile Jackson was still suspended from the game. Given what is known about Jackson and his sense of justice, there is no doubt that once he knew this he would have felt badly treated. If he had been paid by Leicester then they would have been fully aware of his position, but they had got away with no punishment whatsoever. Back in New Zealand, he carried on with his travels oblivious to all of this and still seemed to be playing the two codes, rugby union and Northern Union, off against each other as well as keeping his own options open. Ironically, Northern Union rugby was played on an amateur basis in New Zealand.

In the north of England, a writer for the *Salford Reporter* could not resist poking fun at the whole charade that had unfolded around Jackson, the Leicester club and rugby union in general by composing a verse or two. On 13 February 1909, a couple of weeks after the RFU had delivered its verdict the newspaper printed the following:

"Call me Jones, or Brown, or Smith,
What's in a name, I say?
Provided I am not a myth
And know the game I play.
For then you see, if I don't suit
Or am not satisfied,
Back to Wales I can then scoot.
And with my club abide.

The Rugby Union in our parts
Are keen on amateurs,
When to your game we lose our hearts,
Or when your cash allures,
We are allowed no quarter then,
Their hearts grow cold and hard.
When once I'm in the Lions' den,
With the cash brush I am tarred.

Then of course, I cannot be
A Rugby Union man,
And so it comes about you see
\i must doge them if I can.
I'll say I'm ill where I reside,
And must take a few weeks rest,
If I like your game when I have tried
I'll accede to your request.

But if it is not my desire
To stay up here and play
From Swinton I will then retire

If you don't my name betray.
My club in Wales, of course, will know
And suspend me (I don't think);
If I go back they'll be glad, and so
At my 'badness' they will wink.

This is the latest method out,
By amateurs pursued.
The Rugby Union, there's no doubt,
See through their tactics crude,
But when approached and of this told,
They won't believe it is so.
All that glitters is not gold,
Our men would never go.

But there are none who are so blind
As those who will not see,
And the Rugby Union, you will find,
Are as blind as they can be.
And meanwhile clubs under their rules
Just flout their jurisdiction.
They think the Rugby Union—fools
Who think these evils fiction.

Swinton, two men have got this way,
Within the last fortnight.
And I am told that both their play
For the first time was all right.
Let's hope that they'll improve until
They help the Blues to win
All games they play and help to fill
Swinton's bank with 'tin'."

It perhaps summed up well the feelings of Northern Union fans to the sham approach to professionalism the RFU seem to have adopted. The poem also seems to suggest that it was well known that Jackson had returned to Wales where he continued with his rugby union career.

Many years later, one of Jackson's sons, Irwin wrote to the rugby league magazine, *Code 13* (issue 16), and mistakenly interpreted the decision to clear Leicester of all charges of professionalism as having also cleared his father of the same charges. Nothing could have been further from the truth. Jackson found that out in 1909, but not for a further eight months and only then after he had tried once again to get back into rugby union, albeit via the back door. It would be safe to say that his first love was, and always would be, the rugby union code, but the authorities were pushing him, albeit reluctantly, into the NU camp.

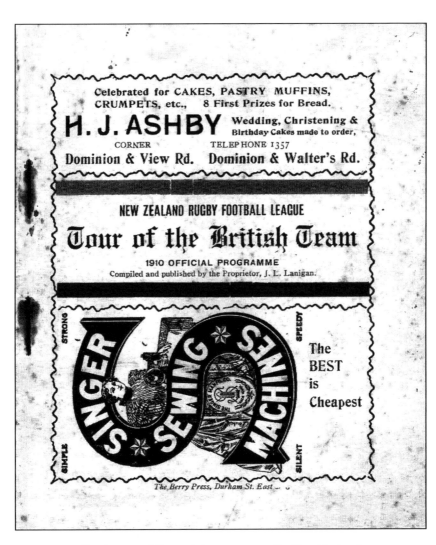

Front cover of the match programme for New Zealand
versus the Northern Union match in 1910.

11. Back to Northern Union rugby

Jackson, it would seem, from the available evidence, continued to flit between the North and South Islands over the next few months. It does appear that he liked to travel by sea because he spent a good deal of time in the Greymouth area on the West Coast of the South Island area and Nelson on the north coast. Greymouth was the centre of a coal mining region which may well explain why Jackson was there. Was he attempting to maintain the pretence of being a mining engineer? There is no evidence as to how he made a living at this time, and sea travel was probably the quickest and easiest way of getting around the country. In his travels it is obvious he was still involved in rugby matters of both codes. As the year wore on and news from England of the RFU's decisions in January had not filtered through, he once again tried to get back into rugby union.

In June 1909 the New Zealand Rugby Union received a telegram from the West Coast Union asking if Fred Jackson could referee a game under their jurisdiction. Jackson must have thought he would test the water by seeing if he could referee. The West Coast Union must have had some sympathy with him because they agreed, but referred the request up to national level. The request caused problems for the national union officials; while they were aware that he had initially been suspended by RFU in London, they were unaware of any further investigation or if there had been any changes to the outcome of that suspension.

They may still have had some sympathy for him and the manner in which he had been treated and may have wanted to assist him, but that did not seem possible. After discussing the matter at length they decided that Jackson was still suspended and therefore could not referee a game under their control. They also took further action by sending a telegram to London asking the RFU to clarify Jackson's position in the game.

It was a decision that was not welcomed or supported by all in the NZRU as the *New Zealand Truth* columnist 'General Gossip' noted on 19 June 1909 when he wrote: "At last week's meeting of the NZRU the question of allowing F. Jackson, a member of the Anglo-Welsh team, to officiate as referee was discussed. Several members contended that as no official notice of Jackson's suspension had been received from the ERU, he could not be prevented from taking part in rugby football in New Zealand. Mr Galbraith stated he had been shown a telegram by Mr Hartnell the manager of the Anglo-Welsh team stating that Jackson had been suspended by the ERU. Of course no one doubts Mr Galbraith's statement, but a telegram is not evidence and is a worthless piece of paper consequently Mr Kelly was right in his contention that as no official intimation had been received of Jackson's suspension, he was entitled to take part in football in New Zealand.

Mr Meredith got heaps of calf wisdom off his chest when he expressed the opinion that the committee had the power to prevent Jackson taking part in football... It is strange the committee which allows the professional rules to be transgressed on its own grounds in seven-a-side games must vent its spleen on a player who has far as the union known officially has nothing against him...."

The article went on to rant about the committee simply 'kowtowing' to the powers that be in London when it suited their purpose while making decisions that are contrary to the rules laid down in England when they wanted to. What the article does show is that Jackson had a good deal of sympathy and support by many inside the game as well as its followers. However, the decision was made to not allow him to referee and to contact the RFU in London.

Once Jackson heard the decision taken by the NZRU he must have concluded that he had no future in the union code. Once the NZRU received official confirmation of his position in the game he knew they would have to follow suit. He therefore set about establishing himself more strongly with the Northern Union code. The *Nelson Evening Mail* wrote on 18 June: "The New Zealand Rugby Union has refused permission to F. Jackson to referee matches at Greymouth. Instead of tooting on the whistle for matches on the West Coast grounds, Jackson will be assisting the Nelson Northern Union players. The League is to be congratulated on their good fortune in having the services of perhaps the finest English forward of today."

To do so was relatively easy for Jackson because there were few players who had actually played the Northern Union game in the South Island. Also, most of Baskervilles' 1907–08 tourists who had returned to New Zealand were based around Auckland. Some had joined clubs in Australia or in the north of England. It was true that Opia Asher's ill-fated Maori tour to Australia and the resulting suspension from rugby union of all those involved had created an influx of NU players, but the numbers were still very small compared to those in the union code.

There was also an added incentive for him to switch codes, namely that rumours were getting stronger by the week that the Northern Union were to tour Australia in 1910 and it was hoped they would add on a visit to New Zealand. With this in mind, on 25 June 1909 it was announced in the press that the New Zealand Rugby League and its headquarters had been established. It was based in Auckland and the new organisation was already in contact with Joseph Platt, secretary of the Northern Union in England. A number of areas in the country had been vying for the honour of hosting the New Zealand Rugby League and Auckland were successful in their application to the Northern Union. The Northern Union in its wisdom decided that New Zealand would be best served if all the other sub-unions had a say in the running of the game, so while ratifying the Auckland application specified that they would not be able to impose their will on the other parts of the country, hence the council was set up based in Auckland.

The rumour circulating the country was that the New Zealand Rugby League were negotiating the terms and conditions needed to bring the tourists to New Zealand. The hope was that six or more matches could be arranged and the tourists would visit both North and South Island. The terms offered were exactly the same as those offered and accepted by the Australians and once NZRL accepted them the tour was effectively confirmed. All that needed to be done was to arrange a suitable fixture list, decide which teams would play and at which venues. Also uppermost in the new body's thinking was how to gain maximum publicity and benefit from the tour.

Jackson, for his part, continued to move between Greymouth and Nelson. He was becoming more and more involved in the Northern Union code. To some extent he was already preaching to the converted in the Nelson area. Newspaper reports said that a good number of players from the Nelson Rugby Union club and others were disenchanted with the union code. In all probability they, like many others in the country, felt that the Northern Union code was better suited to the way they played the game than the old rules. Perhaps they were disenchanted that the NZRU had been unable to convince the RFU to agree to the rule changes they wanted. Whatever the reasons, there was a group of players who had decided that they were going to learn and play the new code.

To that end they contacted Jackson and brought him from Greymouth to teach them how to play Northern Union rugby. More importantly, they paid him to carry out this task and thus Jackson burnt his boats with rugby union in his adopted country. The Nelson players had a number of training sessions which came to the attention of the Nelson Rugby Union officials who were not clear as to what the situation was. Were the players professionalised simply because they were learning the new code? Certainly that would have been the situation in England. However, this was not England and they would decide what to do for themselves. What about the referee and touch judges; were they also tarred with the same brush? Were the secretary of the newly formed outfit and all the other club officials also to be classed as professionals?

There was an added problem for the rugby union officials because the disillusioned players had gone much further than simply trying the new game out. The Nelson newspaper reported that, on Friday 4 June 1909, a meeting was held at the Foresters' Hall in the town at which the new Nelson Rugby League was formed specifically to play the Northern Union game. The proposition to do so was put to the meeting by a Mr R. Kincaid who had not long arrived in the town from Barrow, in the north of England, where he had played the Northern Union code for a number of clubs. At the meeting the newspaper reported that two Northern Union clubs were established, Hornets and Nelson Northern. The newly elected chairman of the league, to assist the two clubs, agreed to supply them with a rugby ball each to practice with. It also seemed that Jackson would act as coach to one club while Kincaid would fill a similar role with the other. There seemed to be little hostility shown toward the new league by the existing Nelson rugby union officials. All the evidence shows that the new league enjoyed a happy and co-operative relationship with their union rivals, who had control of Trafalgar Park, the enclosed ground where the new clubs hoped to play matches.

As the NZRU prevaricated, Jackson continued, along with Kincaid, to organise the new players in their respective clubs into outfits capable of playing the new game. By Saturday 14 August it was not just Jackson who had burned his boats with rugby union, for at Trafalgar Park, Jackson's team took on Hornets in the first ever Northern Union game played in the Nelson district. What was important as well was that the game was played on an enclosed field and gate money was taken from spectators who wanted to watch the action. It was just £3/12/6, but the match resulted in all concerned being banned and branded professional by the rugby union officials, who finally felt compelled to take action. It does seem rather odd that it was this that finally forced them to act because on every Saturday in the season the senior rugby union clubs played on the enclosed ground where people paid an entry fee. By that logic all rugby union clubs could equally have been declared to be professional.

The *Wanganui Herald* on 11 September reported the outcome of the match: "The Nelson Union forwarded the names of 22 players who had taken part in a Northern Union game in that town, also the names of the referee, line umpires and secretary. All these men had been suspended. The suspension was made general and the persons concerned were given a fortnight in which to show cause why they should not be expelled under the rules as to professionalism. The letter from the Nelson Union said that early in the season a Northern Union club was formed in Nelson and several persons under the Nelson Union's jurisdiction joined the club and played in practice matches. No gate money was taken at these matches nor did the players get any benefit in the way of money, with the exception of F. Jackson, a member of the late Anglo-Welsh team, which toured the Dominion last year, who had since been suspended. This man had been brought to Nelson by the Northern Union club to instruct players in the rules of the game".

Thus all those involved in the match were expelled from the rugby union. Jackson would have known that they would be, simply because the *Wellington Evening Post* the day before had published the results of the NZRU's request to London on clarification of his status in rugby union. For Jackson, the game was well and truly up: "A notification was received from the English Rugby Union that F. Jackson of the Anglo-Welsh team, has been declared a professional. It was decided to notify all unions throughout the Dominion."

Jackson was involved in this first ever NU game at Trafalgar Park as the report stated: "Jackson the well known Cornish and Leicester forward led one team." The result was a win for his team. He became heavily involved in the new code both on and off the field, and was elected as the representative for Nelson Rugby League on the New Zealand Rugby League Council in Auckland. The new code was now established in the South Island.

Jackson would have been aware of the rule changes that had occurred in the new code over the years. Clearly Jackson's prowess on the rugby field had not diminished because on Saturday 9 October he travelled to Auckland to represent Wellington in a game which saw the visitors come away with the spoils 22–19. The game attracted around 4,000 spectators and, more importantly, the gate money amounted to around £130. It was money which was vital to the Northern Union cause given the proposed tour by the Englishmen in 1910. Just how or why Jackson came to be playing for Wellington is not known. He was probably the only Nelson player with the ability to perform at this higher level and may have been recruited by the Wellington side to assist them against Auckland.

Outside the game, there was a newspaper report that he was working in the 'state mines' but that was about it. Certainly it would have been difficult for him to hold down a regular job and undertaken the travelling around the South Island that he did.

In spite of all the action at national level against Jackson and the other players involved in the newly formed Nelson League, the relationship between the Nelson rugby union and rugby league bodies remained cordial and co-operative. Often, if one or other code had an important match coming up the other code would stand down to allow the match to be played at Trafalgar Park. Also, they would meet on a regular basis to sort out fixture issues and appeared to work well together to ensure there were no clashes. It was yet another example of the difference in attitude toward the new game in New Zealand and the RFU in England.

12. The NU tour of New Zealand

It would have quickly become obvious to both Jackson and the New Zealand Rugby League that the standard of rugby available in the Nelson League was not high enough, neither was the standard or depth in Wellington. The league needed someone of his quality playing at the highest level and that simply meant the Auckland League. There was an added incentive to bring him to Auckland; he would be on hand to deal with matters arising from the proposed tour by the English Northern Union tourists. The tour had been in some doubt because when the NU had telegraphed financial terms for a tour the newly formed league had replied that it was too early because they had not been established long enough. They felt that they were not yet ready for such an undertaking.

That attitude did not prevail for long because the new union that had been recognised by the Northern Union quickly realised that such a tour was vital to the very existence of their fragile structure. The Northern Union was contacted and told that if a tour was to be made of Australia they would like to extend it into New Zealand. The Northern Union realised the importance of including New Zealand and sent them a telegram with the terms and conditions that they had offered to the Australians. The New Zealand officials quickly agreed and the tour was on. The Northern Union offered to play six matches on their visit and it was proposed that they would visit both the North and South Islands. To the new league this news must have been very welcome. At last they had something to tempt rugby union players to switch their allegiance – the chance to play international rugby in the new code.

In New Zealand, the tour was essential to develop the sport to a higher level. It was vital to keep players in New Zealand and developed a larger player base if they were to survive.

It was true that a good many Maori players were available following Opia Asher's tour to Australia in 1908, but some of them had also been lost to the sport. An added problem had been the untimely death of Albert Baskerville, who had organised the All-Gold tour in 1907.

So the 1910 season saw Jackson plying his trade in the new code in Auckland in preparation for the visit by the Englishmen.

The New Zealand Rugby League began to publicise the upcoming visit and the game took on a new impetus in the country. However, the tourists decided to just play three matches on the North Island, and not visit the South. This was a considerable disappointment to the new code's followers there, and was a missed opportunity to further develop rugby league.

The tourists were to arrive in Auckland on 17 July and the following matches were announced:

July 20: versus New Zealand Maori team in Auckland
July 23: versus Auckland in Auckland.
July 30: versus New Zealand in Auckland.

When the team arrived it was announced that they would not visit the South Island, but would play a fourth match, in Rotorua, against a Maori team.

While there had been discussion about the length of the tour, Jackson was preparing to play international rugby again. He would have been glad to get onto the field after being heavily involved with arrangements connected with the visit by his English compatriots. He was, however, to suffer the same lack of success has he had experienced a couple of years earlier in the other code.

Jackson was selected for the second match of the tour. He was chosen to be in the pack for the Auckland representative side to meet the tourists on the Saturday. The honour of being the first side to meet the tourists on home soil had gone to the New Zealand Maori side who were to meet them four days earlier on the Wednesday. The NZRL officials must have been very disappointed when dawn broke on the Wednesday because the heavens opened. The rain continued through out the morning and on into the afternoon. It was the worst possible weather for the players and officials. All were desperate to put on a good show to impress both the spectators and the somewhat sceptical reporters.

There would have been one slight problem for Jackson when he began preparing for the Auckland game, if not before then. Also selected for the Auckland side was a full-back called Alf Chorley. Chorley was an Englishman who had emigrated to New Zealand in 1908 and, ironically he had played for Swinton in the NU. Not only that, but he had played every game for Swinton in the 1901–02 season, when Jackson was at the club. He would have known Jackson as J.R. Jones and also that this was not his true identity. Did Chorley believe that Jackson was who he claimed he was even now in 1910? Did he know Jackson as Gabe while he was at Swinton? We shall never know...

Chorley had begun playing for the Ponsonby club in Auckland soon after his arrival in New Zealand. He may have been involved in setting up the club along some of Baskerville's returning 'All-Golds'. Chorley

84

played well enough for his club to be selected for not just Auckland, but also the national side. It was strange that their paths should cross on the other side of the world some nine years after playing together at Swinton. What was Jackson's reaction on first seeing Chorley? Equally Chorley would have been aware of the furore that had occurred back in England in 1908. What did he think about Jackson?

Also playing with Jackson in the front row for New Zealand at hooker was Edward Hughes, who had played against him in 1908 when the Anglo-Welsh played the All Blacks in the first test. Hughes then was a Southland forward who was suspended in 1909 by the NZRU for playing club rugby league. He was eventually reinstated by rugby union and went on to represent New Zealand against South Africa in 1920 at the age of 40. He is still the oldest person to represent the All Blacks.

The interest generated by the tourists was shown when 5,000 supporters came to the ground that Wednesday afternoon. They found the playing area almost entirely under water. They witnessed a display from the visitors that saw them come away with a 29–0 victory. What was important, however, was the manner of the win and the rugby played by the tourists in atrocious conditions. The press remembered the visit two years earlier by the Anglo-Welsh rugby union team. They had not treated the tour seriously and had left a bad impression; not so the NU tourists. They were super fit, battle hardened and had one aim in mind: to win. Nothing else was acceptable to them and this impressed the New Zealand players and supporters. Bert Jenkins, one of the tourists' centres, crossed for four tries in a masterful display.

This was achieved on a pitch covered with water so deep that at times it came over the top of the players' boots. The press said that the performance was so good that the other matches arranged were eagerly anticipated. They did not have long to wait.

Just three days later it was Auckland's turn to meet the tourists. Jackson was looking forward to the match and with good reason. Evidence shows clearly that he was to captain the Auckland thirteen against his countrymen.

The rain had never really gone away, but it did not deter the supporters as more than 10,000 made their way to Victoria Park at Freemans Bay to watch the game. The Auckland side took the field in their blue and white strip, contrasting with the visitors' red and white, but they were outclassed, and lost 52–9. One reporter wrote: "The game was fast and exciting throughout, an altogether brilliant exhibition... The exhibition of rugby given by the British team was of the highest class, their combination being excellent. Their passing, running and kicking were well above the New Zealand amateur provincial standard, whilst the tackling of both forwards and backs was of a deadly order. The open passing play raised the crowd to a great pitch of excitement..."

Newspaper reports of the game show clearly that Jackson led the team from the front: "The Englishmen won the toss. Jackson kicked off for Auckland from the western end. Auckland were the first to attack, and the forwards taking charge Jackson made a fine opening and sent to Seagar, who, with a fast dash scored. Jackson failed at goal."

It would seem that in the second half the visitors relaxed and coasted home, scoring only 11 points to the home side's 6; however, the supporters were hooked. So too were the press. This was probably the first time many of the reporters had seen Northern Union rugby played by the code's very best players. They had probably witnessed club matches, but had never seen the game played by players of the tourists' quality and experience. Many of the reporters were converted to the cause of the new code.

Jackson, while failing to convert the three tries Auckland scored, did enough to be selected for the New Zealand test side to play the following Saturday. He would make his international debut for a second time in New Zealand, this time in the NU code and for New Zealand.

As Fred and the rest of the team were preparing for the test match the press were trying to describe what they had seen against Auckland. The only thing they had to compare it to for their readers were the best All Black teams. One reporter said about the visitors: "The English Northern Union player is a totally different kind of footballer person from the English Rugby Union player. He is much superior physically, he can stay out a game better and keep up his end better if things happen to be strenuous This last team, which plays the reformed Rugby, would make the very best New Zealand amateur team ever picked put its very best foot forward to win. Our greatest 'All Black' teams never had a set of forwards who could out-run, out-weight and outwit this side, and their best and liveliest backs could never have shown these men anything to speak of in the matter of accurate passing, fast running, straight and strong kicking and safe tackling..."

Praise indeed from a not unbiased press. The tourists had lived up to the accolades bestowed on them. Could they repeat it one more time in the test, or would the home side put up a better show?

Due to the fact that the tourists were not to travel to the South Island the authorities had hastily arranged a match in Rotorua against a Maori XIII. There is little record of that encounter, but the tourists won quite easily. The newspaper which would have covered the match was the Hot Lakes Times and sadly no copies of the newspaper for that period exist in New Zealand. Other newspapers covered the lead- up to the game, but that was all the coverage that is available at the present time. With the game over, the following day the tourists were back on the train returning to Auckland to prepare for the test match. Jackson and his teammates would have been under no illusion as to what they faced, as were the press. The tourists played the game at a furious pace for the whole 80 minutes. Also, they seemed to be gigantic in physique in every position. Apart from the half-backs it was at times difficult to differentiate who were forwards and who were threequarters. The tourists' captain, James Lomas, looked and played like a colossus and the reporters had probably never seen a centre of his stature before.

As Saturday dawned the weather was at last a little kinder. The League officials were hoping for a bumper crowd at the Domain Cricket Ground and were not disappointed. Neither were the crowd that witnessed a masterful display of the new style of rugby from the visitors. Jackson and his teammates lost 52-20, but were watched by around 17,000 spectators. It was the one and only time the New Zealand team would take the field in a jersey that was red, yellow and black stripes. Why those colours were chosen is unknown, perhaps they were trying to distance themselves from the rugby union All Blacks. Whatever the reason, those colours were discarded for the more familiar black and white for later games against Australia.

Jackson did score this time; he converted three of the tries and also added a penalty. The encounter was not as one-sided as the previous Saturday. The home side more or less held their own in the first half. However, the visitors were just too strong in all departments, and were fitter than the New Zealanders. Jackson was now an international in both codes of rugby and for two different countries.

The Northern Union players in Australia in July 1910 before they travelled to New Zealand for the final part of their tour.

87

Jackson with his hands in his pockets waiting for the kick-off against the Northern Union in July 1910. This was the one and only time New Zealand played with a red, yellow and black stripes shirt.

A couple of days later the tourists sailed for Sydney and life settled down for Jackson, or so it would seem. However, trouble was once again on the horizon for him and his new Maori friends.

It is difficult to say just why he had begun to encompass the Maori culture unless one makes some assumptions as to his true identity, but for now we will simply accept that he did. He was a man with strong convictions and had been on the wrong side of the rugby authorities and felt wronged by them. Perhaps for that reason, the feeling of persecution, he had an affinity for the Maori and their position in society in New Zealand at that time.

Soon after the tourists sailed away, Jackson and his sense of justice came into play and got him into trouble with rugby officials once again. He was in a restaurant with some Maori friends, something that was illegal then, when an official of the New Zealand Rugby League came in. He proceeded to harass the Maori, complaining that they had no right to be there. It would seem that racism was present among some of the white community in New Zealand at that time and the mixing of Maori and non-Maori, or Pakeha as the Maori referred to them, as was frowned upon. When the rugby official got a little too insistent with his demands, Jackson stood up and punched him. It was acceptable for the Maori to play rugby and be feted on the field, but off the field it was another matter and that would have rankled Jackson greatly.

The official reported Jackson to the rugby league authorities and at a meeting on 19 August 1910 he was suspended both as a player and from holding office as a representative for his own league. The minutes of that meeting said quite barely: "Mr F.S. Jackson was removed from office and suspended as a player during the pleasure of the league as per bye law 19." Jackson was once again without a place in rugby football, now it seemed in both codes.

There is quite an enlightening piece of information about Jackson in the *Salford Reporter* on 13 September 1910 when the Northern Union tourists arrived home. The article mentions former Swinton players who played against the tourists for New Zealand, one of which was Alf Chorley. The report said about Jackson: "The other ex-Swintonian in the New Zealand team was the forward locally known as Jones, or the "Mysterious Jones." After leaving Swinton, Jones played for a time in a different name for rugby union teams, and being an exceptionally fine man and a splendid player was selected as one of the forwards who went out to Australia with the rugby union team. In his absence his connection with the Northern Union was discovered, and before the amateur team set sail for home the Rugby Union authorities, dubbing Jones a professional, cabled to Australia suspending him. Apparently he had now thrown in his lot again with the professionals, and in the New Zealand match, he was a distinctly conspicuous figure, not quite so conspicuous as the Salford captain on the English side, but most notable on the other side and especially prominent in the goalkicking department." What the article confirmed, once again, is that Jackson and Jones were one and the same.

Jackson now had the unwanted distinction of being suspended permanently by both rugby codes at the same time. For his part, he seemingly was unrepentant and simply got on with his life. He moved to the coast to an isolated part of the country However, he still could not help cocking a snoot at the rugby officials, this time the rugby union variety. In 1911 he was in Poverty Bay, and had managed to get involved with the Poverty Bay rugby sub-union. On 10 July 1911 the *Poverty Bay Herald* reported on a trip taken by the Poverty Bay team to play the Waiapu sub-union team. The report says that the team and supporters met on the wharf at 5.30am to sail to Waiapu. When on board the vessel: "Many characteristic football yarns were spun, Mr Jackson, who was amongst the local supporters, and who by the way was a member of the British team that played against the All Blacks was in this respect in great form, and kept things merry."

It could be argued that as a supporter he was not breaching any of the conditions of his ban by the New Zealand Rugby Union. However, generally when players were banned they were not allowed to enter any ground under the union's control. What was reported next most certainly was in contravention of the ban as the match report included: "The line flags were held by Messers P. Liddle (Waiapu) and Mr Jackson (Poverty Bay)."

That was definitely in breach of the conditions of his ban, but then it got worse because at the after match reception and dinner many speeches were given and toasts proposed, once they were completed: "Mr Jackson then gave a few remarks on football." In reality, Jackson was the after dinner speaker at an official function of the Waiapu sub-union.

There can be little doubt that the Poverty Bay sub-union were aware of Jackson's status in the game, as is clear from the article on 25 August 1908 in the *Poverty Bay Herald* referred to earlier. It seems that the Poverty Bay and Waiapu sub-unions chose either to ignore the national union's ban on Jackson or were ignorant of it. Either way, Jackson was back involved with rugby union despite being still banned for professionalism. It does again show the attitude of the rugby union officials in the outer reaches and where their sympathies lay. They were squarely with the player.

After this episode Jackson faded into the background as far as rugby was concerned. He left Poverty Bay and travelled to Hastings. He probably would have stayed there were it not for the outbreak of the First World War.

Jackson travelled across New Zealand and in 1912 was in Hastings. There he met a young lady who took his fancy. The young lady in question was a Maori, or to be more accurate a half-Maori. Her name was Horowai Henderson and her father was an Englishman who had been a sheep farmer and like Jackson seemed to have become absorbed into the Maori culture. In all probability, Horowia was a high born Maori or 'royal' and as such was probably light skinned.

Everard Henderson was originally from Worth in Kent and was the fifth son of John and Laura Henderson. His father was a gentleman farmer and also a seemingly thwarted naval man. His own father, Everard's grandfather, had refused him permission to join the service and he was determined not to do the same with his own children. His first four sons joined the navy and all had successful careers.

Their naval records show the following ranks: Admiral Sir William Henderson, Admiral Sir Reginald Henderson, Vice Admiral Frank Henderson and Commander John Henderson.

Young Everard, however, was expected to remain at home and take command of the family farm. By the time he was ready to do so the bottom had fallen out of the farming market in England so he emigrated to New Zealand where he became a very successful sheep farmer. In 1880, he purchased a farm at Whakatane before moving to a 3,000 acre farm at Hicks Bay. It was here that he began to become friendly with the Maori. He set out to learn their language and culture and married a Maori named Ngarangi Kamaea Ngatoko.

Henderson was an influential figure in the area and was looked upon as an elder statesman by the local community. Such was his relationship with the Maori he regularly acted as go-between and translator between them and the Pakeha. The Maori clearly considered him a friend. It was his daughter Horowai that Jackson was attracted to and in 1913 they got married.

On his marriage declaration Jackson once again indulged in a little subterfuge, as did his bride. He gave his father's name as Frederick Stanley Jackson and his mother's name as Mary Louise Jones. To add still further to the mystery surrounding him he declared that he had been born in Leicester. Giving his own name as his father's would not arouse suspicion because this was common at that time. Given that people still remembered him as the Leicester forward from the 1908 rugby union tour, he probably felt it best to simply put that place down on his declaration. As no one was able to check these facts he would have felt safe in doing so.

One other thing which seems to be a little strange was that on the marriage declaration he did not put his real age. In reality he was 35 years old, but said that he was 30. One reason for this could well have been the disparity in his age and that of his bride who said that she was 18. Even stranger is that it seems that Horowai's age was also not correct. All the evidence suggests she was born in 1891 which would have made her 22 when she married. If the idea was to reduce the age gap between the two why would she take three years off her age?

Jackson showed considerable strength of character to marry a Maori at this time. At this time mixed race marriages were frowned upon by both Maori and more so by the Pakeha.

Once married, Jackson and his wife left Hastings with their son Everard and settled back in Te Araroa on the East Coast of the North Island. It was, and still is, an isolated place, but by moving there he may have increased his circle of friends. He may have needed to do so because his non-Maori friends may have wanted to distance themselves from him and his new wife. Also, by moving he would help his wife maintain her ties with the land and her family. So he settled down to life well away from the public eye for a time.

Jackson had been involved with his future father-in-law at least a year or so before his marriage when both were instigators of the establishment of a Legion of Frontiersmen in the Te Araroa district where they both lived. The Legion of Frontiersmen was an organisation set up in England in 1905 by Roger Pocock, a former constable in the Royal Canadian Mounted Police. Its aim was to offer assistance to the government in defending the further reaches of the British Empire. It was set up as a paramilitary organisation based upon Pocock's somewhat romantic view of the frontier and what it entailed. Branches of the organisation sprang up in various parts of the Empire.

However, as events took a turn for the worse in Europe more and more of the countries in the Empire began to set up Legions in various regions. The branch that was set up in Te Aroroa had Everard Henderson as its president, but the secretary was Fred Jackson. His action in becoming the secretary once again shows that he was educated above what would be expected of someone who was from a working class background at this time. It was not the first time he held such an office and certainly not the last. It was this action, which would be a precursor to Jackson marrying Henderson's daughter in Hastings, and also enlisting during World War One, which in turn led to him ultimately being reinstated by the New Zealand Rugby Union.

13. War and back in the union fold

The international political tensions in Europe grew by the week as 1914 went along. Jackson lived in an isolated part of New Zealand and would have got news of events, but that news would be out of date by the time it reached him. As events on the other side of the world moved more rapidly, so the New Zealand people simply could not keep up with them. However, once war was declared in August 1914 the whole of the British Empire would have been galvanised, but slowly. Jackson now happily married. His first child Everard Stanley had been born in 1914; he was working and supported his young family. He would have been disappointed to hear the news, as all were, but he was quick to offer his services to his newly adopted country.

New Zealand, like many other countries in the Empire, had only a small standing army and so would have called for volunteers. They would, however, have been keen to classify those volunteers according to their family and work commitments. Jackson was not accepted for active service due to his marital status and remained at home. As the war progressed so his marriage developed with the birth of his second son, Reginald Tututaonga. Each change took him further away from eligibility for active service. However, as the bloodletting continued at an alarming rate New Zealand, like the United Kingdom, found that they needed to introduce conscription in order to maintain the level of troops needed for the conflict. The New Zealand troops, along with the Australian forces, had seen action on the beaches at Gallipoli with disastrous consequences.

Conscription was subject to certain criteria, which seemed destined to see Jackson remain at home and out of the armed forces. Given the slaughter of many troops in the First World War, this was probably as well for him and his family.

In September 1916 the New Zealand Government ordered that all young men were to register for the ballot, i.e. for conscription. The edict was quite draconian because it stated quite clearly that if a man failed to register then he would simply be ordered to attend for military training and possible shipment over to the war in Europe. Those who registered would be subject to the ballot to see if they were to be called up. Available evidence suggests that Fred had registered of his own accord well before 1916 to serve his adopted country.

As 1918 arrived so did Fred's third son Sydney Freyberg. The war was seemingly turning in favour of the allies and New Zealand, along with others, was called upon for one last push. In June Jackson received his 'call up' papers. He would have been both elated and sad I think. Elated that at last he could help his adopted country, but sad that he needed to leave his family behind. As it transpired he had to do neither. By the time he was conscripted and completed his basic training at the Featherstone Camp, the war in Europe was effectively coming to a close and while in the New Zealand armed forces, Jackson never saw action or left the country. That he was called up by the army did have a life-changing effect upon him, however.

With the war over and New Zealand and the rest of the world trying desperately to get back to normal, the New Zealand Rugby Union made an announcement. They declared that any player, former player or official who had been suspended from the game for whatever reason before the conflict, if they had served in the armed forces would be reinstated if they wished. For Jackson this was the opportunity he had long been waiting for. At last he could return to the game which was, in all probability, his first love – rugby union. He was accepted back into the fold and soon made his presence felt both as a coach, as an administrator and later as an East Coast selector. For now he was content to simply get the game played once more on his home turf of the East Coast.

In 1920 his growing family saw Mary Whati be born and with so many mouths to feed Jackson needed to be working and be reasonably well paid. In 1923 he tendered for the position of wharfinger or wharf master for the Te Araroa jetty. His tender was accepted and he was duly appointed to the position. It is also around this time that yet another facet of his complex character emerges.

A very good friend of his, Doctor Tutere Wi Repa, who was around the same age as Jackson, lost his only son. Wi Repa had, in his day, been a very good rugby player himself and had played for Bay of Plenty against the Anglo-Welsh tourists back in 1908. Sadly, Jackson was suspended and in Australia when the game was staged, but it seems that before the war he and Wi Repa became firm friends. With the loss of his son, Doctor Wi Repa and his wife, as was the Maori custom of the time, asked Fred and his wife if they could adopt Reginald, their second son. Fred and Horowai agreed and Reginald henceforth was known simply as Tutu Wi Repa. This shows the extent to which he had accepted the Maori way of life that he would give up one of his children to help another couple cope with the loss of their son. It must have been a far cry from what would have been expected of an English father, or a Welsh one for that matter.

Once he had been reinstated into rugby union, Bob McConnell's' book *Te Araroa An East Coast Community – A History* shows that in 1920 that he was coaching the Te Araroa Native school team. This is supported by a paragraph in the *Poverty Bay Herald* of 6 November 1920 which said: "The football contests between Te Araroa and Hicks Bay School were concluded on October 25th. The Te Araroa School winning the McClutchie Cup. Not a few of the grown ups are sorry the school football season is over, the matches have been immensely enjoyed. Te Araroa Schools Committee, especially the secretary, Mr F. S. Jackson, who initiated the contests, have every reason for being satisfied with the result."

He progressed from that to coaching many representative teams on the east coast of the North Island. He was too old to play but could coach and was an excellent administrator. For many years he was a selector for the Matakaoa Sub-Union representative team and was instrumental in pushing for an East Coast Union to join the New Zealand Rugby Union.

In 1924, George Rehua entered upon the scene as Jackson and Horowai's fourth son. Finally, in 1927, came the last of their children when Irwin Kotau O Te Rangi was born.

In the 1930s he coached many of the East Coast representative sides. The other thing he was responsible for was choosing the playing colours for the Matakaoa Sub-Union team. Not surprisingly, they played in a red shirt with a broad white band across the chest, the colours of Harding's 1908 Anglo-Welsh tourists.

In the 1930s he saw his own children excel in the sport of rugby union just as he had. His eldest son Everard was selected for the Tokararanga senior team when he was only 14 years old. In 1932, he was selected for the East Coast Representative side and two years later played for Hawkes Bay and North Island. In 1936 he won the first of his six All Black caps and also represented the New Zealand Maori side. John Griffiths' book on International Rugby Records commented that in 1936 and 1937, "...the emergence of a sound and solid front row comprising Jackson, Lambourn and Dalton was an encouraging feature..."

Everard went on to tour Australia in 1938 and was selected for the trial match for the tour to South Africa, but could not be chosen for the party owing to the South African policy of racial discrimination in existence at the time which meant that Maori players could not tour the country. His adopted out son Tutu Wi Repa also became an Maori All-Black as well as playing for the East Coast and his son Sydney also won representative honours although for some strange reason he was always referred to by the press as 'Selwyn'. Irwin, the youngest son, did not reach the same heights as his siblings due to an injury early in his career.

By this time dark clouds were once more on the horizon over in Europe. Germany was lead by Adolf Hitler who seemed bent on righting the perceived wrongs inflicted on Germany after the First World War. In September 1939 New Zealand was once again involved in a conflict on a global scale. Fred was quick to offer his services to his adopted country and joined the Home Guard. He quickly rose in the chain of command owing to his excellent administrative skills. He even arranged for his youngest son, Irwin, to join the Home Guard at the tender age of 14.

When the war broke out Jackson's three eldest children enlisted in the 2nd Maori regiment and served with distinction through out the war. Sadly Everard was wounded and lost a leg. He spent the rest of his life in pain and never fully recovered from his wounds. But all three survived the war and returned home, much to Jackson's relief. The war over, the family simply wanted to get back to normality as did most people.

Later Jackson left Te Araroa and settled in Auckland where he lived out the rest of his days. His youngest son Irwin, writing in the original *Code XIII* magazine, and his grandson Moana Jackson, both say that Fred was very reluctant to talk about his life prior to 1908. No doubt he had his reasons for this, but sadly on his death in 1957 none of his immediate family knew what his true identity was, and obviously what their own ancestry really was.

Moana Jackson, his grandson, put it into perspective when he said that he simply remembered a warm loving man who was a great person to be around and that "A little mystery serves only to burnish the memory of my grandfather."

Not only were the family in the dark about aspects of Jackson's life and identity prior to 1908, but so were rugby union world and rugby league. He was a mystery to historians of either code and as time passed so the memory and interest in Jackson faded. That was until I wrote a book chronicling the exploits of the first ever rugby league tourists to Australia and New Zealand back in 1910, *Best in the Northern Union.* Even then, Jackson was not on my radar until a simple sentence in a long email from a rugby historian in Australia started me on long quest to unravel the mystery of Frederick Stanley Jackson. That led to the solving of a mystery that had defeated people for over

100 years. It involved researchers working in New Zealand, England and Wales to solve the mystery. Nothing in this book so far confirms Jackson's true identity, although his feats on the rugby field are portrayed.

Equally what is written here is what has been pieced together from newspaper reports over in New Zealand and here in England from books and journals along with minutes from the Rugby Union committee meetings of the period. It provides an insight into Jackson's life. The twists and turns in the road that I went down in solving the mystery of just who Jackson really was are yet another story in themselves.

Jackson is in the flat cap, with the Tairawhiti representative rugby side on 3 September 1939, the day the Second World War began.

The last resting place of F.S. Jackson and his wife Horowai.

14. The investigation

The starting point for this book and subsequent investigation into Jackson's life came from a previous book that I had written about the first ever tour to Australia and New Zealand in 1910 by the Northern Union. On that tour the Northern Union played a test match against New Zealand in Auckland. One of the New Zealand forwards that afternoon was Frederick Stanley Jackson. While I was checking the facts about the Australian leg of the tour with Sean Fagan, the Australian Rugby League historian, in an email he included a pretty innocuous sentence to the effect that "Jackson was an interesting character, he went to New Zealand with the 1908 Anglo-Welsh tourists and never returned home."

They say from little acorns great oak trees grow, similarly from that single sentence grew this whole book. As any rugby historian will say, when provided with such an intriguing statement further investigation is irresistible. That sentence set in motion a chain of events that would eventually see a mystery that had existed for over 100 years solved. The email caused me to read as much as I could, to find out what was known about Jackson. The mystery deepened even further when I discovered that to all intents and purposes he had never existed. Or, more accurately, his true identity seemed no longer to be known by anyone today just as it had been unknown back in 1908.

All that has been written up to this point in the book is an account of Jackson's life, some of it based simply on newspaper and sporting magazine articles written at the time these events took place. None of what has been written actually provides his true identity. What follows is an account of the long investigation that had the specific intention of attempting to uncovering the true identity of Frederick Stanley Jackson. There are a good many people who contributed to the work of tracking Jackson down to his birthplace and indeed his birth and my eternal thanks go to each and every one of them. They in no small way contributed to the unravelling of this mystery.

His life was rather like an onion, as I unwrapped one layer another one appeared then another and another, I never seemed to get to the bottom of the mystery. Not only that, but each uncovered layer seemed to add to the mystery rather than offer clues to a solution. When the investigation began I decided to start from what we knew and develop from there. What was not in dispute was that he had been selected for the 1908 Anglo-Welsh tour down under and that he had given as his name Frederick Stanley Jackson. A New Zealand newspaper had published an, albeit, brief pen pictures of the tourists and in Jackson's case he claimed to have been born in Camborne in Cornwall. He also claimed to have been educated at Camborne School of Mines and as a result was a mining engineer. This was a pretence he maintained for quite some considerable time. In the New Zealand records of men eligible via the ballot for war service he is listed as a mining engineer from 1914 through to 1922. One could be forgiven for mistaking Camborne the town and Camborne School of Mines as being related to each other. In actual fact the school was and still is an annex of Exeter University. I am sure Jackson would not have enlightened people to any of this.

None of what at that time he claimed about himself would appear to have been true because it seems it was checked out at the time the furore about him erupted way back in 1908. However I decided to recheck to see if the situation remained the same 100 years on. After all, I had no way of knowing if the checks reporters claimed they had carried out had actually been made. They did and they had, there was no record in the census for Cornwall of a Frederick Stanley Jackson being born around the time he claimed. There was no record of a Frederick Stanley Jackson being born anywhere in the county at that time that came even close to matching his profile. When contact was made with the archivist of Camborne School of Mines an extensive search of their records revealed that no one of that name ever attended the school. Jackson had claimed to have played both cricket and rugby for the school, a search through the year books for the period told a different story, there was no record of Jackson. So it seemed the investigations as conducted down in Cornwall by the newspapers and reported on in 1908 were correct. The question then was what next, where do you go from there?

It seems an obvious choice to then move onto the reasons why Jackson was actually recalled from the tour. Had he really played for the Northern Union club Swinton and if so was the name he used of John R. Jones really true or false? In order to investigate further I contacted Graham Morris, a rugby league historian who was well versed in the rugby clubs of Manchester and Salford. While confessing not to be an expert on the Swinton club he knew a man who was, namely John Edwards who had researched the club's early history.

He was my next port of call and he informed me of what he had unearthed about Jackson. Intriguingly, he confirmed that Jackson had signed for Swinton and had used the name John R. Jones, but that it was something of an open secret around the club that it was not his

100

true identity, merely a 'football identity'. The other thing John did was to share freely with me the results of his own research and a number of newspaper articles he had managed to salvage many years before when the original newspapers of the period were about to be consigned to a rubbish skip.

It was one of those articles that unlocked another avenue of investigation for me as it was revealed a possible date of birth for Jackson, something at that time and even today which was unknown, even to his own family in New Zealand. The article in question was an interview with him for the local Swinton newspaper in September 1901. It revealed that he claimed he was 22 years old. Depending on when he was born that could mean a year of birth of either 1878 or 1879. Armed with that information I was able to go back and research the census of 1881 for Cornwall once again with the same negative results. The article, however, also revealed two other important facts that could be investigated. First, he claimed to be Welsh and born in Morriston; and that he had seen action in the Boer War in South Africa.

There was also evidence that had emerged at the time of his recall back in 1908, that while purporting to be Jackson, he was in fact a Welsh man by the name of Gabe. The Leicester secretary, Tom Crumbie, had in December 1906 been forced to admit that Jackson and Gabe were one and the same. The evidence from 1901, 1906 and also 1908 seemed to suggest that there may well be something in the Gabe aspect of the mystery. I decided to investigate that avenue further. Once again in the 1908 investigations into the claims made that he was Gabe, born in Morriston and educated at Llandovery College by the newspapers, were investigated, it would seem there was no supporting evidence for those claims back then. I attempted to investigate the known facts to see if I got the same answers that reporters had obtained way back in 1908, sadly I did.

There was no record of a Gabe born in Morriston in the Swansea area around 1878 or 1879 on the census that matched what was known of Jackson. Similarly checks revealed no such person named Gabe from Morriston had been educated at Llandovery College. Given that I had no idea as to his true identity it seemed improbable that an investigation into a Gabe or Jackson serving in the Boer War would prove successful. I had no name and no idea what regiment he had or had not enlisted in, even though he claimed in the interview in 1908 to have joined as a private and then gained a commission, but it was stated he had joined a Transvaal regiment. The investigation seemed destined to stall at this point just as it had all those years ago as

101

information about Transvaal regiments was almost impossible to obtain for that period.

The next line of enquiry seemed to me to be to return to his time at Swinton. Jackson himself never admitted or denied this at the time of his suspension. He claimed instead that he had no knowledge of why he had been suspended by the authorities. Research does show that there can be no doubt that the man did play for Swinton, or should that be John R. Jones did? Reference to both the *Salford Reporter* and *The Journal*, of the period, both of whom covered the Swinton club at that time shows this quite clearly. Jones appeared on the scene at the club just after the start of the 1901–02 season. There is a reference in *The Journal* of 30 August 1901 which says the club had made five new signings, however Jones was not mentioned as being one of them. The first reference using the name Jones I found was in the *Salford Reporter* on 14 September when their writer said: "...the team for the home 'A' team match (Stockport 'A') includes A.N. Other. A.N. Other will probably turn out to be a 22 year old 14 stone recruit named Jones from Cardiff. If so it is calculated that the natives will be startled."

It seems that there was little point in rugby union players using an alias if they played a trial match for a Northern Union club, when the reporters in the north were printing their names for all to see. The reporter did however do us a favour as his words confirm that Jones was playing for the Swinton club.

Further confirmation, were it necessary came in *The Journal* of 4th October when it published the following: "Amongst a long list of registration permits by the Northern Union this week were the following for Swinton. John Jones (Gordon's Cape Town)." Jackson would have needed a permit to play due to the fact that he must have missed one or two days work in the week leading up to the game on Saturday. If a player was injured and as a result missed going to work even for a day then the league authorities needed to sanction that he was allowed to play. In fact if a player did not work the Wednesday, Thursday and Friday prior to Saturdays' match they were not allowed to play. It was important to the Northern Union authorities to show that players were not living on the match fees they received for playing, but had to also work to be able to live.

Just a day later the *Salford Reporter* wrote: "[The Northern Union Committee] sanctioned Barnett's registration with Swinton along with J Jones the new forward described as of Cape Town."

Both of these references support the view that he had been in South Africa at the time of the war, something he maintained through out his lifetime. It would also seem to confirm that he had crossed the equator prior to doing so with the Anglo-Welsh tourists in 1908. It was not until the 21 October that there is any reference to Jones and his exploits on the field of play. Once again it was the *Salford Reporter* in a report of the 'A' team game, this time at Stockport. The reporter wrote: "Apart from Traynor the interest of the spectators centred chiefly on the appearance of J. Jones, the new forward from Cardiff, who has now thrown in his lot and a big lot it is, with the Dark Blues. He is built on much the same lines as Harry Eagles or Alf Teggin and there is a further resemblance in the amount of verve he puts into his play."

Strangely, there seem to be no further references to him in match reports and so on until the season was drawing to its close. However, I suppose that being a forward his exploits would not be reported on as freely as that of a back would have been. It does seem strange that if Jones did make his debut against Hunslet in a match that Swinton won 10–7 that no reference was made to his performance. It could have been expected that the reporter would have let the reader know how he had performed on his debut. Sadly, he did not and did not mention him again during his 13 first team appearances until he played his last game for the club. The *Salford Reporter,* writing about the first team's cup quarter-final match against Broughton Rangers at Wheaters Field on 4 May 1902 said in the report of the first half of the game that: "...game was stopped owing to Jones being hurt and this player was carried off the field and play continued without him."

Just a few sentences later in the report he continued: "Jones limped back into the field of play but it was very easy to be seen that he played under great difficulty during the rest of the game."

That would appear to have been his last match for the club as *The Journal* a few days later, previewed the last game for that season and said that Jones, who was injured in the Broughton match, was not to play. By the time the new season was about to begin there is no mention of him at the Swinton club and no explanation why he was missing. I have no idea what or how serious the injury was that he sustained, but what is clear is that he left Swinton never to return, going back to what was probably his first love, rugby union.

If, as I suspect, Jackson deliberately chose the initials of J.R because of the fact that there was another forward G.R. Jones, and he hoped to confuse anyone attempting to identify him then he was successful.

The Rugby League Record Keepers Club 'Blue Book' that records all players at a club that played in a particular club side certainly fell into the trap that Jackson laid. When one looks at the 1901–02 season for the Swinton club we see only J. Jones playing in the pack for the club and playing 18 games. Deeper investigation through John Edwards however shows clearly that J. Jones shown in the records was in fact both J.R and G.R Jones, but had been recorded as J. Jones. In truth John Jones was to play just 13 games for the club. Jones does seem to follow one Jackson trend, however. He would disappear from the rugby scene for a few weeks and then reappearing. His appearances apart from toward the end of the season are a little spasmodic. Sadly, all this information did little to lead me any nearer to uncovering his true identity and yet another avenue had come to a disappointing end. However, what he did have was three aliases that had been used at one time or another namely, Jackson, Gabe and Jones

I decided on what I thought at that time would be one last throw of the dice and made an attempt to contact Jackson's family living in New Zealand. With that aim I got in touch with John Coffey and Bernie Wood two respected journalists and rugby league historians, the latter put me in touch with Jackson's grandson, Moana Jackson. Sadly it seemed Moana Jackson and the family as a whole knew little if anything more that I had managed to unearth other than to confirm that his grandfather had in fact married a Maori girl, so I was back at square one, but did have a new Maori angle to explore.

Through John Coffey I made contact with a genealogist and rugby enthusiast named Yvonne Chisholm. Yvonne had been of help to both John and Bernie in establishing the true identity of players from the early days of the Auckland Rugby League for a book they were writing about the Auckland history. She was able to come up with new information previously undiscovered by rugby historians in this country. This new information added to the known knowledge, but seemed also to lead only up one blind alley after another. One such alley was when from Jackson's marriage declaration form in New Zealand I got his parents names. The marriage declaration form in New Zealand is much more useful than the marriage certificate as the person must give a great deal more information about themselves.

The odd thing was that he claimed on his marriage declaration to have been born in Leicester rather than Camborne or Morriston. There was no surprise when he stated that his father was named Frederick Stanley Jackson as he would, it was common for children to be named after their father then but his mother's name he gave as Mary Louise Jones. When I saw that my senses pricked up, had he actually slipped up and given the true identity of his mother? At the same time as this information came to light similar information was obtained via another source, Jackson's own family, that showed they claimed their grandmother's name to be Marie Louise Jones, I had the Welsh connection, albeit tenuous, to say the least, of Jones. The search of the census proved fruitful as there was a Marie Louise Jones in London in 1881. She was working as a nurse domestic at a private school in Islington North London.

For the first time I began to get excited and felt I was beginning to get somewhere. London fitted the known facts, that Jackson claimed to have played for the London Welsh club and secondly that the reporter who interviewed him in Manchester had formed the opinion that Jackson was educated well above that expected of a normal working class man. Had he been educated in that private school by the man who was the principal, Septimus Payne under whose roof Marie Louise Jones was living in 1881? If Jackson were her illegitimate son then I could well have solved the mystery. Certainly had his father been a wealthy man it would explain how Jackson had been able to travel to South Africa as a young man. Sadly, it proved not to be the case and I had gone down yet another wrong track in the search for Jackson's true identity. There was no evidence of an illegitimate son being born to Marie Louise Jones in any census records for the time and the London area and yet again the trail faded out.

As one trail faded away another one became more illuminated because I changed tack yet again for the "umpteenth" time and asked myself the question why had Jackson actually married a Maori? It was known that he had been suspended by the New Zealand Rugby League for assaulting a league official who had upset his Maori friends so there was an affinity to that race of people, would it lead anywhere? At that time mixed race marriages would not have been common by any means so it would have been a very strong couple that undertook such a marriage.

I started with his wife Horowai Henderson and looked at her background it quickly became apparent that she was only half Maori. Her father was in fact an Englishman by the name of Everard Henderson from Worth in Kent who had moved out to the Dominion in the 1880s. The Henderson family was quite a colourful one to say the least and once investigations into them began, once more I saw my hopes of finding the answers soar. Everard was the fifth son of Joseph Henderson and his four elder brothers were destined for the navy. Joseph had been desperate to join the senior service, but his father had forbidden him to do so. He was determined not to thwart his sons

105

in a similar manner ensuring the four of them enlisted. There they all made considerable names for themselves, two rising to the rank of Admiral and were knighted. The other two became a Vice-Admiral and a Commander, a good tally for four siblings.

It was, however, the youngest daughter of the family that caused me all the excitement, for she was reported by her present day relatives, allegedly, to have given birth to an illegitimate son! Could this be the youngster that was Jackson? Investigations unearthed a boy being born in 1878 in Greenwich in Kent who was named Frederick Stanley H Henderson. Given that the Henderson family name included the name Hannam and this was usually abbreviated to a simple H, It was not unreasonable to assume the H in the child's name could well be Hannam. Also, as an unmarried mother and the daughter of a wealthy landowner it was common at that time that she would have been 'sent away' to give birth in order to lessen the shame. Hence the child being born and registered in Greenwich rather than Worth. Attempts were made to obtain a copy of the birth certificate in the belief that this was Jackson and that he had indeed married his first cousin, something not unheard of at that time. But when the birth certificate duly arrived it was the end of yet another false trail and another blind alley. The mother of the child was not the Elizabeth Henderson I was investigating.

By this point in the investigation I was beginning to lose heart and believed that Jackson's secret died with him. It was a case of going back over old evidence and seeing if something had been missed. I also decided that I would put together an article complete with a photograph of Jackson and email it, along with a covering letter, to the sports editors of the local South Wales newspapers. I did so in the hope that if the newspapers published the letter and that there was some truth in the claim that Jackson was actually Gabe a relative who may be alive would read of him and make contact with me. It was a very long shot as we were talking of events that occurred over 100 years ago, but at least I felt I was doing something rather than giving up on the quest.

While I waited for something to develop on the newspaper front I began re-reading the old newspaper articles looking for any clue that I may have missed first time around. While doing so I read an article in one of the New Zealand papers of the time that gave me a fresh impetuous. It was a reprint of an article first published in the *Athletic News Weekly* in England and then reproduced in New Zealand and commented upon by the local rugby writer. The article had been written at the height of the 'Jackson scandal' so was relevant at least to the time frame. The article mentioned the fact that Jackson had actually played for the York club prior to them joining the Northern Union in 1898. There was nothing new in that as an article that John Edwards had given to me earlier had mentioned the same thing and referred to Jackson as being 'Trooper" Gabe. What grabbed my attention was the following sentence in the New Zealand paper that was not in the article John Edwards had given to me, which stated that Jackson/Gabe was "One of the death or glory boys."

This was something I had missed completely first time round or, more accurately, had probably not attached much importance to it. I wondered who or what was a 'death or glory boy'? Once more I went back to the internet to see if I could throw any light on the quote. To my delight I discovered it was the motto of what is today the Queen's Royal Lancers, could this actually be the regiment that Jackson had served in and fought in South Africa? If he were in a Lancer regiment it was not unreasonable to assume that he could or would have been referred to as "Trooper", after all that was what he was. He maintained all his life that he was a Boer War veteran, could this really have been the case? I was able to establish that the regiment which at the time Jackson would have served in was the 17th Duke of Cambridge's Own Lancers had been in South Africa from 1900 and fought in the latter days of the Boar War. Investigations with the present day Queens Royal Lancers regiment regarding Jackson or Gabe proved fruitless as they did not keep the records of individual soldiers and they directed me to the archives at Kew Gardens in London. I hoped the investigation would develop if I confirmed that the regiment had served in South Africa and the Boer War.

As is always the case when carrying out research of this nature one struggles to establish a fact, but once it is established further proof seems to appear. This is the case here for later research unearthed evidence to support the claim. The *York Herald*, 21 January 1896 carried the following article: "York's new man, Gabe, who is one of the "Death or Glory Boys" might adopt that motto as a footballer. He used to play for Swansea; and he gave promise of turning out a useful acquisition to the York team on Saturday. It would be unfair to further criticise his play; as he has not appeared in the field for some time and he was evidently very stiff."

If that were not enough evidence to support the view that Gabe was a Lancer, a week earlier the following had appeared in the same newspaper: "J.G. Gabe of the 17th Lancers stationed at York was, like

H.W. Rhodes, picked as one of the team early in the week but was unable to turn out. He used to play for a South Wales club..."

It seems that the initials J.G were used, just why is not clear, but then Jackson was never much bothered by names it would seem. What is certain is the name Gabe was not a common name in that part of the world. As I said if further evidence was needed that Jackson was a former Lancer the above would support that.

Sadly, as seemed to be the case in every avenue I explored, this proved to be more difficult than one would expect. When I approached the National Archives I was informed that all members of the army from before 1922 were subject to their army pension entitlement status. In the record book referred to as WO97 all those who were entitled to an army pension generally speaking were listed and in many cases their service history was on file. Sadly if the soldiers were not entitled to an army pension their service records had been destroyed. Given it was highly unlikely that Jackson would have applied for such a pension it was reasonable to assume his records no longer existed.

I once more returned to the Queens Royal Lancers regiment and this time had a little more success. Given that Jackson always claimed to have been a veteran of the Boer War then he should have been entitled to either the Queen's Medal or King's medal because they were the two awarded for that conflict to soldiers who had seen action. The regimental archivist's office very kindly carried out a search of their medal roll to see if there was any record of Jackson. Initially I asked if there had been an Ivor Gabe in the regiment as I felt perhaps he could have enlisted under that name. It came as no surprise when the answer came back no such name was on the roll. I then asked if there was a Frederick Stanley Jackson on the medal roll? When the search looked for Jackson there was more success.

If we accept that he was in the army then it could explain why he appeared in later life to be 'better educated than the average working man' as the Manchester reporter claimed in 1901. At that period the British Army was attempting to improve the education of the private soldiers it recruited. To this end it in many cases provided education for the troops and if Jackson took advantage of such an offer then certainly his education would have been greatly improved as we have seen it was. It would also be a logical explanation as to why, during his time in New Zealand, he took on the role of secretary of a number of organisations as well as running his own business as wharf master at Te Araroa in the 1920s. The problem I had however was that he was listed in the army as F. Jackson. That being the case I was still no nearer solving just what his true identity really was.

After having waited a number of weeks to see if the article I had sent to the South Wales newspapers would throw up any new information, sadly without success, I was again losing hope. Quite frankly I had all but run out of ideas and alleys to explore, I was about to give up hope of ever moving forward. I was coming to the conclusion that I would never solve the Jackson mystery, I suppose there was no disgrace in that after all he had defeated the journalists and investigators of 100 years ago. That at a time when the evidence was fresh, and people involved at the time could be questioned, what chance had I got today when the trails were over 100 years old? Jackson had weaved his web of deception so well it was proving as impenetrable today as it had in his own lifetime

As is usually the case, however, having resigned myself to giving up the ghost, out of the blue came new information, information I had been searching for, for over a year or more. I received an email from a man named Glyn Gabe in South Wales. Incredibly he claimed to be the nephew of Fred Jackson and had read the article I had sent and that had been printed in the *South Wales Evening Post* that weekend about Jackson and my request for information. It had taken the newspaper over six weeks or more to get round to publishing my request. Glyn Gabe claimed that Fred Jackson was the 'black sheep' of the family who had been ostracised because he had 'gone north' to play professional rugby. This, he said, was according to information he had been told as a youngster by his uncle who was Jackson's younger brother. Glyn Gabe was 93 years old!

The information he supplied matched the details of the known facts, facts which had not been put in the article in the newspaper and so not for the first time I got very excited, was I at last going to solve a mystery over 100 years old? Glyn Gabe's family actually went to the census records in their library after speaking with me on the phone and there further unravelled the mystery. It seems Fred Jackson or should that be Ivor Gabe was in actual fact neither. He was born **Ivor Thomas Gape** in the Morriston area of Swansea on 24 August 1877. He was the second son of a Thomas Gape who was at the time of his birth a tinplate assorter in the Iron and Tin Works in the area. More importantly his mother is named as Susannah Gape née Jones. It would seem that Jackson may well have been telling the truth in part at least when completing his marriage declaration form back in 1913.

109

The 1881 Welsh census for Glamorgan confirmed this, listing him as a three year old. The reason I or the reporters back in 1908 could not find him on any census was that we were all looking for the wrong name. He was actually born GAPE, ironically as had Rhys Gabe, the famous Welsh centre who played at the same time as Jackson, who as further research and information from Glyn Gabe confirmed, was a cousin of Jackson. Rhys Gape's father and Thomas Gape, Jackson's father were brothers.

Rhys Gabe had a very distinguished career in Welsh rugby union. According to Fields of Praise, David Smith and Gareth Williams' official history of the WRU, he was born in Llanegennech in 1880, and after playing for village teams and Llanelli Intermediate School, played for Llanelli. In 1903 he became a schoolteacher in Cardiff and had a long association with the Cardiff club. He played for Wales in their famous victory over the All Blacks in 1905. He made his debut for Wales on the wing, but mainly played at centre. Interestingly, he also played for London Welsh, when he was doing teacher training at Borough Road College. He toured Australia and New Zealand with the British Lions in 1904, and died in Cardiff, aged 87, in 1967.

By the 1891 census in Wales the family had change the name to Gabe and Jackson is shown as a 13-year-old now working as an apprentice pattern maker in the same iron and tin works close to Morriston that his father worked in. I have not been able to establish if the family name was actually changed legally, but the Swansea branch of the family told me what happened. It would appear that there was another Gape family in another part of Swansea that had no connection to them. In order to avoid any confusion between the two families it was decided to change the name from Gape to Gabe. Whatever the reasons for the change the family at some time between 1881 and 1891 became known as Gabe and are known by that name today. This would also lend more weight to the view that the well-known international rugby union referee Gil Evans expressed that he had known Jackson as Gabe while he was at school. Evans was teaching in the Swansea area at the time Jackson would have been at school.

These facts also suggest a reason why we could find no record of a Gabe playing for Swansea at the time it was claimed he was doing so. In the village of Morriston in the 1890s the Morriston Rugby Union Club, which is still playing today, was quite a strong club. They played fixtures against the likes of Swansea, Neath and Cardiff. Perhaps Jackson had played his early rugby for the Morriston club in the Swansea area.

Left: John Gabe, Fred's brother.
Right: Fred's brother Glyn Gabe who was the father of the Glyn Gabe who made contact with me following a newspaper article in the *South Wales Evening Post.*

In this group at the back with the watch chain is Doctor William Gabe, Fred's other brother.

The Jackson brothers: S.F. (Bully) Jackson, Everard Jackson and R.T. Jackson (Tutu Wi Repa). Photo: Irwin Jackson

111

Hence people referring to him as the 'well known Swansea forward'. Research in the local papers for the period failed to throw up any clues about his playing career. The newspapers covered only Neath, Llanelli and Cardiff, not Morriston.

Further investigation unearthed information that would support the view that Jackson left Morriston without completing his apprenticeship in the Iron and Tin Works. The Swansea newspaper of the time, *The Cambrian,* covered a story in September 1892 stating that the Works was to be closed at the end of that month. It would seem that the American President McKinley had introduced a number of tariffs on imports. One such tariff had been placed on the import of tin plate and as a consequence the bottom had fallen out of the tin plate market in South Wales. The Works did in fact close on 28 September 1892 just a month after Jackson's 15th birthday.

While efforts were made in November 1892 to partially re-open some of the works perhaps Jackson as an apprentice was expendable. Certainly he would have seen little or no future for himself in Morriston which to a large extent relied on the Works for employment. It could well have been that seeing the writing on the wall he decided to get out the only way he knew, through the army. Being under age but maybe looking older than his years Jackson may well have joined the Lancers. It was a requirement at that time with a Lancer regiment to sign on for eight years, and he used the false name of F. Jackson. I cannot say if his actions met with the approval of his parents, but I think probably not hence the use of the name F. Jackson when he enlisted rather than Ivor Gabe. Had he enlisted around late 1892 he would have completed his service in late 1900 or early 1901. This would fit the time line for him returning to this country and rather than return to his family in Morriston where he perhaps would be less than welcome, he went to Manchester and joined Swinton.

There is, however, another somewhat darker explanation for Jackson's departure from Morriston. His nephew Glyn Gabe recounted the story he had heard from his uncles that one of Jackson's younger siblings had returned home from school having been punished by his teacher. Jackson, it seemed, took exception to this and returned to the school and hit the teacher. Such behaviour would have not been tolerated by either the school or the law and if it had gone to trial and he had been found guilty, would have resulted in a prison sentence. Perhaps it was this incident that caused Jackson's hurried departure from home and into the army under an assumed name. Whatever the reason, Morriston had seen the last of him.

From 1892 or 1893 it would appear that the army took over, all the evidence suggesting, for whatever reason that he took the King's shilling joining what is now the Queens Royal Lancers and did serve in South Africa. There is evidence of this from four separate sources namely the article in 1908 when the secretary of Broughton Rangers talks of Jackson being 'Trooper" Gabe who played for York around 1897, an interview he gave to a Manchester paper in 1901 when he claimed to have fought in the South African war. Then there was some seven years later an interview he gave on the Wellington dockside in 1908 when he was leaving for Sydney having been recalled to England. Finally the article in the *Otago Witness* reprinted from the *Athletic News Weekly* published in Manchester claiming he was a 'death or glory boy'.

Adding to this evidence the information that the family in New Zealand have then the view that Jackson served in the Boer War is strengthened still further. Writing in the early 1990s his youngest son Irwin said, "For reasons of his own dad was very reticent of his past before 1908." He went on to say that he remembered his father speaking of Boer War service, but that was all. Irwin Jackson had written to *Code 13* (issue 16), following an article by Graham Williams in issue 13 entitled "Alias Gabe and Jones" which was a preliminary study of Jackson's life and the issues that led to his suspension from the tour.

Interviewed in 2010 by Yvonne Chisholm, Jackson's daughter Mary also confirmed what Irwin had said, she said that her father had talked of serving in South Africa. She also claimed he could have been wounded and that was the reason he used a stick in later life. Given this information I wonder if it is an explanation why he regularly missed two and three weeks of playing during his career? Was he actually suffering from the wounds he received in the war in South Africa? She also said that he hated canned corn beef as that had been the staple diet of the soldiers in the Boer War. In conversation Mary said, as had other members of the family, that her father's life prior to 1908 seemed to be a closed book. Yet she did reveal tantalising tit-bits of information that add to the overall picture that had been built up of Jackson's early life. For example, she said that her father used to make lava bread which is both a Welsh dish and it must be said an acquired taste. He was also fond of making oat cakes with slivers of bacon around the edges, again a typical Welsh dish. One is prompted to ask why should he make such Welsh delicacies unless he had eaten them as a youngster back in Morriston?

In 2011 Yvonne Chisholm went to Gisborne and interviewed a man who knew Jackson when he lived at Te Araroa. During her meeting with Sandy Hovell a number of facts emerged, unsolicited facts it must be stressed. His recollections of Jackson were: "Fred always turned up very neatly or well dressed in a grey sports coat, dark pants and a tie for this duty. Sometimes he also had a flower in his lapel." Sandy remembers this fact so well because his parents had the closest house to the field and he used to take Fred a cup of tea and cakes made by his mother at half time. He confirmed Fred's booming voice, agreeing you could hear it all over Te Araroa. Fred collected the entrance money and the money always balanced, people couldn't sneak past him.

He went on to recall that Fred: had a limp and walked with a stick; had a horse and was a capable rider; was a strong man physically; had a good singing voice; knew "quite a lot" of the Maori language; went game shooting and was a good shot; "barracked" loudly at rugby matches and lived in Pohatu Road.

While all of these facts lend weight to the argument that Jackson, Gabe, Jones and Gape are one and the same man, further proof if it were needed came when Sandy recalled that Fred did not have an English accent like the other English people in Te Araroa and that he thought Fred's accent was Welsh.

Many of the facts Sandy reveals suggest a man with military training in his past; his riding skills could well have been learned while in the Lancer regiment. It is also interesting that both he and Mary refer to a leg injury perhaps. It is however, the accent which strongly suggests that Jackson was from Wales and if that is true then the Gabe/Gape connection becomes even stronger.

What is incredible is that at the age of 13 he was an apprentice pattern maker so his schooling would have been rudimentary and yet by the age of 21 or 22 he was described as having more than the average working man's education. As we have seen while in his adopted country he became secretary of quite a number of different organisations and did the job very well, like 'a natural' in fact. Perhaps he was self educated or genuinely did have a natural talent for the written word. One thing is certain he was an extremely clever man and self made at that.

Further correspondence with Glyn Gabe and his family in Swansea lead to him and his wife Val supplying me with a number of photographs of the family. In particular they had photographs of who they said were Fred's brothers, John and Glyn and William. Fred himself was notoriously difficult to photograph prior to 1908, however later photographs of him were able to be compared with the Gabe family snapshots. The family resemblance is striking enough to enable one to feel quite confident to say that they are brothers. Jackson really is, I feel, Welsh and was born as Gape.

Further research carried out in early 2011 unearthed yet another facet to the mystery. It seems that his older brother, William Gabe, was also an accomplished rugby player. The newspapers from the 1890s for the Morriston area reveal that he often played for the Morriston club, and was also a goalkicking forward. More importantly, he also played on many occasions for the London Welsh club. Perhaps it was he who unwittingly provided the information regarding the workings of Llandovery College to his younger brother. We know that then, as now, many of the players for that club came from the Llandovery College.

Researching the national newspapers also proved successful and *The Western Mail* on Monday 4 March 1895 carried a report of the rugby match played the previous Saturday between Morriston and Aberavon. In the article the reporter named the two sides taking part and named as playing in the forwards for Morriston was Ivor Gabe. If further proof were needed that that it really was 'our' Ivor Gabe it came later in the report: "Dan Jones was penalised, Ivor Gabe making a good shot for goal."

There is no doubt that Ivor played in the same Morriston team as his older brother, perhaps people had mistaken Morriston for Swansea as they were very close at that time.

If, as evidence suggests, Fred Jackson did play for the club and London Welsh on their tour of the south east of England it is not stretching probability to believe that contact could have been made with him via his brother William. It is the only strong connection I have found between Jackson and the London Welsh club.

What has been unearthed to date tells us that we now know he was born Ivor Thomas Gape on 24 August 1877 and that at some stage in the following 10 years the family name was changed to Gabe. Whether this was done legally or the family just simply decided to use the name Gabe rather than Gape we shall never know. Why did he seek to change his name and then hide his true identity even from his own family here and in New Zealand? That again we shall never know.

What exists is a paper trail of evidence which is so strong that it becomes very difficult not to believe that Jackson is who I claim him to be. There is a birth certificate in the name of Gape and information from the family in Wales that this name was changed to Gabe some time between 1881 and 1891. We have evidence that 'Trooper Gabe'

115

played for York prior to 1898 while they still played rugby union. In December 1906 the Leicester secretary Tom Crumbie was forced to admit to the professional sub-committee that he knew that Gabe was the real name of Fred Jackson. There are players and officials who admitted to the professional sub-committee once the story was made public in 1908 that they knew Jackson was 'the Swansea forward Gabe' and some admitted they also knew he was Jones, the Swinton forward. Finally there is an article in the *Salford Reporter* that Jackson and the J. Jones that played at Swinton were one and the same person. I am convinced that Jackson's true identity is **Ivor Thomas Gape**. However if one huge gap in our knowledge of Jackson has been filled not all the gaps have been as successfully answered.

That other annoying gap in all of the research evidence and which also is unanswerable is simply how did he fund himself during his playing career? How could he afford to go on tour with the Anglo-Welsh team, support himself for 12 weeks or so in Sydney and return to New Zealand? How did he raise the funds to travel extensively around New Zealand when there is practically no evidence that he was actually holding down a job. Certainly in New Zealand it would have been impossible for him to hold down a job and yet take so much time off as he appears to have done, unless of course he was secretly being funded by Northern Union sources as an 'organiser' for that code, that also we shall never know.

One other possible explanation could be that he was injured during the Boer War and as a result was awarded a pension from the army. It is hard to believe that such a small sum as a pension of this nature would provide could finance his rugby both here and during his time in New Zealand.

What has been achieved by this investigation is the solving of a mystery that has given me and others a great deal of personal satisfaction having spent over a year researching for the answer. Namely just what was the true identity of rugby's 'mystery man' Frederick Stanley Jackson? More importantly it will give closure to some of his remaining family over in New Zealand, although it must be said that opinion in the family is split with regard to whether or not the evidence uncovered proves who Jackson really was.

Moana Jackson and his branch of the family in New Zealand are sceptical of the evidence that has been unearthed. Their scepticism comes from the fact that research has failed to unearth any photographs of Jackson prior to 1908. The truth is that Jackson was extremely difficult to photograph and if as I feel he did come from a poor Welsh family would that family have the wherewithal to afford to have a professional photographer take family portraits? The photographs we do have are of his brothers and there is without doubt a striking resemblance between them and Jackson himself.

Mary, his daughter, also is unsure as to whether Jackson really was Gabe. The New Zealand side of the family will remain, I assume, Jacksons, but will know that their name could well be Gape or more realistically Gabe. Although they would still argue that people are confusing the Ivor Gabe purporting to be their grandfather with Rhys Gabe the famous Cardiff centre of the same era. I, however, feel the evidence is so strong that Rhys Gabe can be eliminated from the picture. Rhys Gabe was very well known in Welsh rugby circles, and apart from a spell in London doing teacher training, lived his whole life in South Wales.

The Welsh side of the family will remain Gabe and continue as they have done for the last 100 years or so. That is to say they believe that all the evidence uncovered proves that Fred Jackson is Ivor Gabe who was born Gape and is the son, brother and uncle who left Morriston in 1895.I would hope that both sides of the family if not pleased with the outcome will welcome the additional information about Jackson contained in these pages. I sincerely hope that all those rugby historians who have played a part in solving this mystery are as pleased as I am with the results. To all other rugby historians of either code I hope they will make a reasoned judgement based on the evidence uncovered. To the reader I would simply ask that they consider the evidence and then make up their own mind as the whether the mystery of Fred Jackson has been solved, or not.

I suppose the last words to describe the man who was Fredrick Stanley Jackson, alias John Jones, alias Ivor Gabe, alias Trooper Gabe alias Ivor Thomas Gape are best left to a quote from the great Winston Churchill which could well be applied to him. He was:

"A riddle wrapped in a mystery inside an enigma."

117

The paper trail

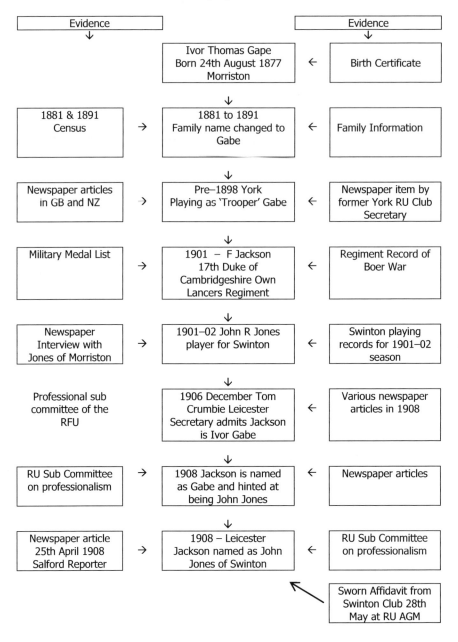

Evidence		Evidence
	Ivor Thomas Gape Born 24th August 1877 Morriston	← Birth Certificate
1881 & 1891 Census →	1881 to 1891 Family name changed to Gabe	← Family Information
Newspaper articles in GB and NZ →	Pre–1898 York Playing as 'Trooper' Gabe	← Newspaper item by former York RU Club Secretary
Military Medal List →	1901 – F Jackson 17th Duke of Cambridgeshire Own Lancers Regiment	← Regiment Record of Boer War
Newspaper Interview with Jones of Morriston →	1901–02 John R Jones player for Swinton	← Swinton playing records for 1901–02 season
Professional sub committee of the RFU	1906 December Tom Crumbie Leicester Secretary admits Jackson is Ivor Gabe	← Various newspaper articles in 1908
RU Sub Committee on professionalism →	1908 Jackson is named as Gabe and hinted at being John Jones	← Newspaper articles
Newspaper article 25th April 1908 Salford Reporter →	1908 – Leicester Jackson named as John Jones of Swinton	← RU Sub Committee on professionalism
		Sworn Affidavit from Swinton Club 28th May at RU AGM

Appendix 1: Significant matches

Jackson's only rugby union international match.

The match was played on Saturday 6 June 1908. The match report is from the *Taranaki Herald* of Monday 8 June and reads:-

A magnificent game
Dunedin

The first test match between New Zealand's chosen fifteen and the British touring team of 1908 was played on the Carisbrook ground today. The weather was fine and the ground in splendid condition. The teams were as follows:
Britain
Full-back: Jackett, Three-quarters: Gibbs, Vassall, J. "Ponty" Jones, J.L. Williams, Halves: Davey, Laxton, Forwards: Harding (captain), Dibble, Oldham, Ritson, Down, Archer, Jackson, Kyrke.

New Zealand
Full-back: Colman, Three-quarters: Cameron, Mitchinson, Thompson.
Five-eights: Hunter, Stead, Half: Roberts, Wing-forward Gillett.
Forwards: McDonald, Seeling, Francis, A. Wilson, Cunningham, Casey, Hughes.
New Zealand won the toss and played with the wind the wind, Britain kicking off with the sun in their eyes. The New Zealanders immediately rushed play into British quarters, where a free kick to New Zealand saw Roberts pilot the ball over the bar, drawing first blood for New Zealand.
New Zealand 3 Britain 0
Immediately after the drop out Thompson streaked for the line and succeeded in penetrating Britain's defence, scoring a brilliant try. Roberts converted.
New Zealand 8 Britain 0
Play hung in mid-field for some time, then Mitchinson broke away in an attack, and beating the British defence scored another try for New Zealand. Gillett converted.
New Zealand 13 Britain 0
New Zealand were having all the best of the exchanges. Playing a very disparate game, their forwards hustled the British forwards and backs and rolled the British backs on the defence. Once again New Zealand swarmed to the attack, Cameron on this occasion getting over in the corner. Gillett again converted from a very difficult angle.
New Zealand 18 Britain   0
The New Zealanders were holding the upper hand and shortly after from a loose scrum Roberts dashed over on the blind side. Gillett failed with the kick.
New Zealand 21 Britain   0
At the change of ends the breeze which had prevailed in the first half died down to a whisper. In the opening stages of the second half Britain rolled the

New Zealand backs on the defence, but could not get through with the fliers of their three-quarter line. New Zealand now came at Britain, and Roberts nipped round the blind side of a scrum. Gillett failed with the kick.

New Zealand 24 Britain   0

Britain rallied, and put New Zealand on the defence for a while. In mid-field Davey snapped the ball out to J.L. Williams who sent it on to "Ponty" Jones. The latter transferred to Vassall. The famous Oxonian raced down the touchline at great speed to the New Zealand goal supported on his right by Gibbs the Welsh International, who took a flying pass at top speed and swerving past Colman scored a brilliant try, which Jackson converted.

New Zealand 24 Britain   5

After the kick off the New Zealand forwards rushed play into the British quarters where Hunter succeeded after an elusive run in getting over. Robert's kick at goal failed again.

New Zealand 27 Britain   5

New Zealand attacked again and the ball flew across the British goal line, where the bounce beat Gibbs. Mitchinson rushing in picked up the ball and dropped over the line. Francis converted, and so a sensational game ended.

New Zealand 32 Britain   5."

It is worth noting that the Seeling that was playing in the New Zealand pack that day was Charlie Seeling who was to sign for Wigan in 1909. In the 11 seasons he played at Wigan he made 226 appearances scoring 76 tries. His son, also called Charlie, also played for Wigan for 10 years from 1933. He made 86 appearances and scored 11 tries and 10 goals before transferring to Warrington.

Jackson's last rugby union match

Fred Jackson played rugby union for the last time on Wednesday 21 June 1908 just three days before the telegraph suspending him arrived from London. The opponents were Nelson and Marlborough and the match was played in Nelson. The *Evening Post* on the following day printed a report of the game which was to turn out to be his last recorded appearance under rugby union rules. The report read:

The following were the teams:-
British: Full-back: Jackett, Three-quarters: Gibbs, McEvedy, Ponty Jones, J.L. Williams, Halves: W. Morgan. T. Jones, Forwards: Dibble, Jackson, Morgan, Downs, Green, Ritson, Archer and J. F. Williams

McEvedy won the toss and the British played with the sun at their backs. Smith set the ball in motion. Ponty Jones returned and Green broke away, but was pulled up for off-side play. Good dribbling by McDonald shifted play to the British twenty-fives, where the visitors got a free kick for unfair scrum tactics. A good mark for the local men by Richmond was nullified by off-side play, but a long kick by Smith and a mistake by Ponty Jones enabled Nelson to attack. Tuan Jones relieved after some indecisive scrumming but O'Brian returned splendidly. Smith next obtained a mark, from which Saunders made a good but ineffectual attempt, Jackett forcing after some amusing by-play.

Nelson still attacked and one man got across amidst great cheering but was called back. From the scrum W. Morgan centred and further scrums followed. Abortive passing rushes were attempted by the visitors. A good kick by Saunders set the Britons on the defensive and the Nelson backs gained twenty yards by pretty passing. The forwards pressed close to the line till a free kick enabled Jackett to clear.

Nelson returned, Jackett being hard pressed, but getting the ball out mid-way by magnificent kicking. From a scrum the Nelson backs, by fine passing, came close to the British line, but further passing lost them ground. Off-side play by Hannigan brought the Britons relief, and Gibbs was instrumental in establishing a British attack from the visitors twenty-five.

Smith lead a fine rush to opponent's territory, but here J.W. Williams saved with a timely run and kick into touch at the centre. Sandel sent the leather back, and through hard kicking the Britons were compelled to force. A period of interesting open play followed, neither side gaining much ground till the Nelson backs again got away with a smart passing rush, Ponty Jones kicking into touch in the nick of time. The visiting forwards then livened up and headed by Ritson carried the ball to Nelson's twenty-five, where as a result of a bad pass by Morgan, Tirrill dribbled to the full-back; Jackett returned to half-way.

The Nelson forwards were not to be denied, and came down the field in a fine rush. Their backs also at this stage showed up much better than their opponents, whose passing was continually breaking down through faulty handling. Good work by Tuan Jones enabled his side to make a brief invitation of Nelson territory, but fine kicking by Manning, and unfair placing of the ball in the scrum nullified the advantage and loose play in the centre of the field followed till just on half-time, when the British were again defending.

Second spell

Dibble set the ball in motion for the second spell and smart work by Ponty Jones and Gibbs saw the visitors attacking the latter making a fine attempt at goal from half-way. After the kick out, Morgan passed smartly to Tuan Jones who sent on to McEvedy, who by a fine dodgy run almost got over. The Nelson forwards relieved the pressure, but Gibbs from a free kick found touch near the Nelson line. Here Saunders, by the best kick of the day, sent the ball sixty yards down the field. The local men by good forward play, kept the ball in the enemy's quarter, and the attacking backs attempted a passing rush, which failed at the critical moment through off-side play.

From loose work near the centre, Gibbs sent the leather to McEvedy who beat his man, gave to Ponty Jones who transferred to Williams. The last named, by a dashing run bored across the line and scored at the corner. Gibbs failed with the kick.

121

Britain 3 Nelson 0

Smith set the ball going, but Tuan Jones returned beautifully and later stopped a dangerous forward rush keeping the ball in local territory. Hot scrimmaging followed here till J.F Williams receiving a sharp pass from Morgan went through the ruck and scored near the line. Jackson failed with a difficult kick.

Britain 6 Nelson 0

From the kick out, Saunders was prominent, and by good kicking found touch near the opponents goal.

A smart local forward rush nearly went over the line, and Smith, from a mark made a good kick, which fell short. Ponty Jones, McEvedy and Gibbs, instead of forcing, carried the leather by fine passing well down the field, but Saunders was again equal to the occasion and returned well. A Nelson passing rush at this juncture looked dangerous, but the British forwards with the best dribbling of the day came right down the field in a body. McEvedy nearly got over from a scrum after this, and off the return kick from a mark Jackson piloted the ball over the bar.

Britain 9 Nelson 0

Nelson rallied, and after give and take their forwards went down near to the line in fine style, Jackett finding touch at the twenty-five. The attack was continued for some time, but the British forwards were now playing better and worked up to mid-field. Again fast forward rushes by Nelson returned the attack, and the British backs had an anxious five minutes till Tuan Jones got the ball away to the centre. Here the visitors pushed the local men fully fifteen yards in a scrum, and a fine bout of passing between Tuan Jones and Gibbs saw the latter thrown into touch when making a dangerous streak for the line.

The Nelson backs centred the ball, but the Reds were now throwing the leather about, and a fine bout of passing was spoilt by Ponty Jones hanging on too long. From a loose scramble near the line the ball went into touch in goal. Two free kicks brought temporary relief to Nelson, but Gibbs, by fast following up, again brought danger. Costello relieved, but after a couple of ineffectual passing rushes, in one of which McEvedy was well grassed when in a dangerous position, Ponty Jones came through the Nelson backs and scored, Jackson failed with the kick.

Britain 12 Nelson 0

A free kick enabled Nelson to attack, and Costello receiving a pass, went hard for the line, but was thrown into touch by Gibbs at the twenty-five flag. Time was sounded with the score:-

Britain 12 Nelson and Marlborough 0."

It was perhaps not the departure he would have wanted, but then at the time he had no idea that it would be the last time he would pull on a jersey to play rugby union.

Jackson captains Auckland against the NU tourists

Northern league game
Auckland badly beaten

"The British team played their second match of the tour at Victoria Park this afternoon, when they met the Auckland representatives. The weather was showery and there was a large attendance. There was an absence of sun and wind.

The Englishmen won the toss. Jackson kicked off for Auckland from the western end. Auckland were the first to attack, and the forwards taking charge Jackson made a fine opening and sent to Seagar, who, with a fast dash scored. Jackson failed at goal.

The game was very fast, travelling up and down at a great pace. From a sensational passing run, Jenkins broke through, and scored. Lomas converted.

England's game was very fast and open. Auckland attacked for a space, but the Englishmen eventually got going. A loose dribbling rush ended in Jukes falling on the ball. Lomas goaled.

Auckland rallied, and the Englishmen forced. England were giving a good display and Auckland were continually on the defence. Davies set his backs going and Avery scored the third try. Lomas was again successful with the kick.

The next try came immediately afterwards, through the agency of Riley. Lomas failed to kick the goal.

Auckland made a dash, but it was only a temporary rally. The visitors attacked again, Leytham adding a try. He goaled.

England 23 Auckland 3

The game was very fast and exciting. England's passing was wonderful. Tries were added by Riley (2), Jukes, and Kershaw, three of which were converted by Lomas. At half time the score was:-

England 41 Auckland 3

Second half

The visitors were immediately on the attack from the kick-off, but Auckland cleared, and set up a hot attack. The visitors defence was severely tested, but was solid, and they had no difficulty in repulsing the invasion. Auckland were making a much better showing than in the first spell. The pace however, was being maintained, the Auckland forwards in particular putting dash into their work. Jenkins, the full back for England, worked brilliantly, saving his side time after time. Eventually the Auckland attack proved successful. Smith, making a fine opening, sent to Asher, and the latter shook off Riley and Jenkins, and scored amidst applause. Jackson failed with the kick.

England 41 Auckland 6

Auckland now put a lot of heart into their work, but the visitors retaliated, coming away with a brilliant dash, and Lomas dribbled over and scored. Rich failed with the kick.

The locals were more than holding their own with the Englishmen, but play lacked finish, and hard tackling nullified the efforts of both sides, which were forced in turn. Then Nolan put Auckland on the attack by a tricky feinting run, but England retaliated and Winstanley scored. Lomas converted.

Auckland were soon defending again, and Leytham scored near the corner. The kick failed.

Auckland made a final rally and Griffin scored. The kick was resultless, and the game ended.

England 52 Auckland 9

The attendance was estimated at 10,000. A light rain fell in the early part of the game, but the weather cleared up shortly after play commenced.

The game was fast and exciting throughout, an altogether brilliant exhibition."

Jackson's last NU representative match

New Zealand verses England
(Played at The Domain in Auckland Saturday 30 July 1910)
Auckland Evening Post (1 August 1910)

The match English team v. New Zealand Northern Union's representatives was played on the Domain Ground this afternoon. New Zealand played with a strong sun and light breeze behind them. After a short series of exchanges, Seager made a fine opening, and New Zealand attacked first, and continued on the offensive until England forced. After a spell of lively play between the halfway and English line, Batten opened up cleverly, and set his whole team moving in a passing rush. Jenkins crossed the line, and grounded the ball, but was called back for a throw forward. England continued to attack, and eventually Smith got possession, sent to Thomas to Leytham, who scored, after a good run at the corner. Lomas failed with the kick at goal.

England 3 New Zealand 0

New Zealand rallied on resuming, and a free-kick allowed Jackson to register a beautiful goal.

England 3 New Zealand 2

The New Zealand forwards were holding their own, and the visitors were not displaying the brilliancy of last week. Eventually England were awarded a free-kick, and Lomas kicked a goal.

England 5 New Zealand 2

New Zealand caused some excitement by setting up a lively attack. Buckland scored and Asher failed to goal.

England 5 New Zealand 5

Encouraged by the success, New Zealand again attacked, and McDonald scored.

New Zealand 10 England 5

The game was now fast and the home team was showing surprisingly good form. Leytham got away, but E. Asher caught him from behind, and the chance was lost. England kept up the attack, and Avery scored, Lomas converting.

England 10 New Zealand 10

The New Zealand forwards were holding their own, and counteracting the work of the English backs. After both sides had taken part in an exciting attack Seager scored.

New Zealand 15 England 10

On resuming New Zealand made things lively, but from his own twenty-five Jenkins broke away, and looked like scoring. Chorley averted the danger with a splendid tackle. The New Zealand forwards relieved the pressure with a fast forward rush, but the strong running Englishmen brought the leather back to the line, and Sharrock picking up smartly, potted a beautiful goal.

New Zealand 15 England 12

The New Zealand forwards rushed the ball to England's twenty-five, but their play was faulty, and England returned the attack, Chorley and E. Asher saving cleverly. England were not to be denied. Mason starting a passing run, Smith got over. Lomas failed with the kick.

England 15 New Zealand 15.

England came back to the attack, and were now showing all their true form. The game was fairly even till gradually the New Zealand defence was beaten down. Kershaw, with a clever bit of work, scored. Lomas failed at goal.

England 18 New Zealand 15

This was the turning point in the game. England added quickly to their scores, the tries being secured by Leytham and B. Jenkins 2, in quick succession, one of which was converted, and the score read.

England 29 New Zealand 15

New Zealand were making a plucky but ineffectual, fight, and after another brilliant passing run, Lomas scored and converted.

England 34 New Zealand 15

The next score came from a forward scramble, Avery being the try getter. Lomas converted.

A second afterwards another fast run ended in Thomas scoring. Lomas again converting.

England 44 New Zealand 15

Shortly after, from another spectacular run, Avery scored. Lomas failed with the kick.

New Zealand made a final rally, and after a lot of loose forward play, Hughes scored and Jackson converted.

England 47 New Zealand 20

Only a few minutes remaining to play, but t was sufficient time to enable Kershaw to score. Thomas converted, and the bell rang with the scores,

England 52 New Zealand 20

It s estimated the attendance was fifteen to seventeen thousand. The game was another bright exhibition, and interest was maintained to the end.

Jackson's' last match for Swinton
Broughton Rangers versus Swinton
(From *The Salford Reporter* 12 April 1902)

Previous games between the Lions and the Rangers have always produced keen encounters and this match was no exception to the general rule. With regard to the previous rounds in the cup both teams had proved excellent in defence, for Swinton had only had six points scored against them, and the Rangers nine. The Lions had scored 53 points and the Wheater's Field contingent only 33, but it must be remembered that the Rangers had throughout met stronger teams than Swinton, and consequently they had had fewer opportunities of making big scores. As far as league games are concerned both teams could claim an equality, as each had beaten their opponents on the latter's ground. The Rangers defeating the Lions at Swinton in October by three points to two, whilst Swinton succeeded in beating the league champions at Broughton in February by eight points to three. In fact Swinton are the only team to have managed to thrash the Rangers on their own ground this season. The following are the results in the various cup ties:-

First round: Broughton Rangers 15 points, Keighley 7 points; Swinton 2 points, Halifax nil. Second round: Broughton Rangers 5 points, Stockport nil, Swinton 17 points Morecambe 6 points. Third round: Broughton Rangers 13 points, Hull 2 points, Swinton 34 points, Whitehaven Recreation nil. The Rangers were slightly the better favourites for the match, although there were not a few who believed Swinton capable of repeating their performance on the occasion of their last visit. The Rangers committee were fortunate in being able to select the same fifteen players for the match that had done so well against Hull on the previous Saturday. Swinton on the other hand had to make an important alteration, Bob Valentine, the captain being unable to assist his side owing to injuries he received in the Morecambe match, when his ankle was badly damaged. It was thought he would be able to turn out but the doctor forbade it. Vernon Hampson was still on the injured list and Messer and Bwere therefore drafted into the threequarter line. During the interval of waiting for the commencement of the match the Irwell Street Mission Band played several selections.

A cheer went up when it was seen that Williams had won the toss, and Evans kicked off for Swinton. Wilson returned to Davies who marked. From a kick Swinton quickly attacked and the first scrimmage was formed well in the home quarters. Upon the ball becoming loose Hogg shone with a good run and kick but off side lost ground. Within five minutes good work by S. James ended in the play passing to Wilson who raced over amidst applause. Sam James kicking the goal. This early and unexpected success encouraged the Rangers who quickly returned to attack, and the Lions were next penalised. Oram failed

126

at goal, a minor being the only reward. After the drop out good work by Messer forced the Broughtonians back. Here some good passing was indulged in by the visiting backs, and Widdeson tackled Cooper in fine style. Good kicking by Wilson followed, and play ruled at centre, until a fine burst away ended in Stead crossing the line, but the whistle had gone. Upon resuming Barnett broke away in fine fashion, but he knocked on in trying to gather again after he had kicked, and a grand chance was gone. Marks by Messer and Oram followed, but the Rangers now compelled their opponents to fall back, and a moment later the Blues were penalised for off side, and the consequent was the next pack was fought out near the Swinton line. Harry was next prominent for the home team but a free kick for off side brought Swinton relief. Winskill put in a good run, and the home side again forced matters, and it was with difficulty that Swinton kept their lines intact. The Rangers were playing a remarkably good game and maintained the pressure until a fine concerted movement by Davies, Messer and Barnett drove them back to their own quarter. Chorley had defended well on several occasions prior to this attack, which was maintained with much vigour, Davies and Morgan being very prominent. Evans was given off side and the visitors lost a lot of ground as the result. Swinton now played much better, and by short stages reached the home twenty five. Loose work by the visiting backs was next seen. Evans was once more off side. Operations next raged near the Swinton line, but Chorley saved nicely when pressed. Still the bulk of the play was carried on in the visitors half, and Wilkinson scored after neat passing between S. James and Harry. S. James failed at goal, the kick being a difficult one considering the sodden condition of the ball. With this strong lead the home side played a capital game, and the visitors had all their work cut out to prevent further disaster.

From a scrimmage in front of the Swinton posts Barrett the ball nicely to S. James, who easily beat the Swinton defence and scored under the cross bar, the same player converting amidst loud cheers. The game was next stopped owing to Jones being hurt, and this player was carried off the field and play proceeded without him. Notwithstanding this the visitors worked their way into the home portion but Wilson was very safe, and with a long telling kick drove play to half way. Jones now limped back into the field of play, but it was easy to be seen that he played under great difficulties during the rest of the game. At half time the score was:- Broughton Rangers two goals, three tries 13 points Swinton, nil.

On changing ends Whitehead kicked off for the Rangers, Wallwark returning to Stead, who had his kick charged down. Trotter was next prominent with a mark, but still the centre became the scene of play, both teams trying their utmost to breakaway, but the brilliant tackling on each side was too keen. A brilliant save was affected by Harry, and a good run was made by Wilson, who however placed his foot into touch. The Swinton forwards gained possession from several scrimmages, but to no purpose as first one and then another of the Swinton backs failed to stick to the ball which was certainly in a very slippery condition, Morgan perhaps being the worst offender. Gradually the home side over played their opponents and Davies and Morgan were kept busy defending, the Broughtonians playing a winning game. Jones made a good mark for the visitors but Wilson caught the ball well from the kick and passed to Hogg, who was not grassed until he reached the corner. Keeping up the pressure, Wilson kicked over the line, and Whitehead dashed up at top speed, but he was just too late, Chorley kicking the ball dead just as the former was in the act of falling on it. Swinton were now a beaten team and play was rarely out of their half at this period. Pollitt next saved his side by marking, but Wilson returned with a similar performance, and still operations raged in the visitors' quarter. After this Swinton exerted much pressure and time after time looked like getting over. Remarkably good defensive work, however, kept them out, the tackling of the Rangers being exceptionally keen. Messer intercepted a pass intended for Widdeson and ran to the home quarter line where in attempting to dodge Fielding, he slipped and thus a grand chance was lost. Swinton made repeated and strenuous efforts to score, and Fielding exhibited fine form at full back. On one occasion Morgan made a dash a few yards off the line, but Fielding tackled him superbly and lifted him off his feet. Chorley at the other end was equal to all emergencies, and several times checked movements, which seemed likely to end in the Rangers increasing their score. Barnett also exhibited fine form, and several times made gallant saves. Davies for Swinton initiated many movements which looked like reducing the lead of the home team, but time after time these were nipped in the bud and time was called with the Rangers still in a majority of 13 points to nil, no score having taken place in the second half of the game.

Appendix 2: The Tigers' feat: Leicester Tigers and the RFU 1895 to 1914
by Graham Williams with Peter Lush

In the period covered by this book, Leicester Tigers survived and thrived in rugby's middle ground between professional and pristine amateur. The club represented, depending on your perspective, either a glittering prize or a critical bastion in the battle between the amateur and professional factions in English rugby.

Over the 20 years following the birth of the Northern Union (NU), the Leicester club occupied a crucial place in the evolution of the relationship between the two games. From the RFU's perspective, Leicester stood practically alone as an example of how a loyal, commercial gate-taking club could prosper in its world, despite the suspicions that surrounded it and the restrictions that were placed upon it. For the RFU, Leicester was its most northerly major club and it was critical that it was not only defended, but strengthened. In return for that defence the Leicester Tigers stayed loyal, no matter what affronts to the club's dignity the RFU inflicted on them.

For the supporters of the NU, the Tigers appeared a natural recruit to the world of competitive professional rugby, especially as their need for gate receipts drove team-building activities that seemed at odds with the RFU's amateur regulations. Yet when approached the Tigers' officials seemed unwilling or unable to recognise the advantages of joining the NU. Somehow neither the NU nor the Northern Rugby League (NRL) was able to turn the opportunity that Leicester presented into a vibrant presence in the midlands. Was that failure primarily down to the northern game's weak business basis?

Was it only on the basis of the RFU expelling the Tigers, something a minority strongly advocated, that the NU could have persuaded them to join?

Thomas Crumbie, Leicester's secretary during the key events covered in this book, was born on 1 February 1868. He had little experience as a senior player. He played mostly for Leicester Swifts, who were County Senior Cup winners in 1890–91, on a few occasions for Leicester 'A' and on three occasions for the Tigers' first team. He quickly discovered his real talents lay as an administrator, first as an officer of the Swifts, before becoming county secretary in 1892 and later secretary of the Leicester 'A' team. He was elected honorary secretary of the Tigers on Friday 2 August

1895, aged 27. Crumbie resigned as honorary secretary of the County Union to become honorary treasurer, which he was for two years.

Crumbie ran his own stationery and printing business on Halford Street, Leicester. Some accused him of being dictatorial and he was certainly both loved and feared by many. His commitment to the Tigers was immense; he ran the club's day-to-day business, organised the team and ran the line on most match days. In summer Crumbie was actively involved in local athletics – he ran the Tigers' Sports and regularly acted as a gate steward for the Infirmary Sports. His printing business churned out programmes for many local sporting events. It was also responsible for printing handbooks for many local sporting clubs and bodies. Crumbie's enterprise and enthusiasm carried him into the heart of Leicester's sporting world.

He had inherited a club that was yet to enjoy real success. In an effort to overcome that lack of honours the club had been using methods of team building that were very similar to those used in the north of England. A town the size of Leicester with engineering, footwear, hosiery and knitwear industries could easily provide jobs for leading players if it wished. Recruitment of that kind had been the spur for investigations to be launched by the RFU in the north and had led to a series of high profile suspensions, which started with Huddersfield in October 1893.

By summer of 1895, Leicester Tigers' first team was a well-assembled blend of a dozen midlanders plus a trio of journeymen from further afield. Among these journeymen was Edward Redman – a forward formerly with Manningham who made his debut on 16 September 1893. Redman had moved south to become a licensee at the Welford Tavern in the town and served as Tigers' captain in both 1894–95 and 1895–96. Redman should have won an England cap, but was forced to withdraw through injury after being selected to play against Ireland on 6 February 1892. He was an England reserve in 1893, but was ignored by the selectors after that.

Also in the team was Bob Hesmondhalgh who made his debut on 26 November 1892. A centre, formerly with St Helens, who joined the NU in 1895, Hesmondhalgh was originally from Ambleside in Cumbria. Playing alongside those two northerners was Billy Foreman who made his debut on 7 October 1893. Foreman was a half-back, who came to Leicester with Kent Wanderers in 1893 and was allegedly found a job as a mechanic by Tom Crumbie. He switched allegiance and played for Midland Counties in 1894–95. Foreman later became a publican in the town. Also, Leicester had employed a professional trainer, which was very unusual then.

It is likely that the Tigers' leading members contained a mixture of staunch amateurs, some who wanted to see a more liberal amateurism introduced and some who were in favour of professionalism, although not all of those would necessarily have supported the NU.

Less than a month after Crumbie's appointment the world of English Rugby Union was thrown into turmoil when, on Thursday 29 August 1895, the Northern Union was formed. There was little, if any, overt sympathy in the midlands for the NU or its aims. Perhaps in recognition of that situation the rebel Union had defined its southern boundary along the ancient line of the River Trent, which excluded practically all of the midland counties. For some reason the NU rescinded that decision at a meeting on 17 October – perhaps because of enquiries from clubs in the midlands about membership if the RFU took action against them over professionalism.

The only immediate impact of the split on the Tigers came once the honorary secretary decreed on 3 September that as far as the RFU was concerned the secessionist clubs were suspended for being in breach of the professional laws and therefore "... no club belonging to our Union will be permitted to play matches with any club which has membership of the Northern Union."

That decision meant the Tigers had to cancel their season-opening tour to Warrington and Stockport. The return fixtures against those two clubs also had to be cancelled out as were planned fixtures with Huddersfield and Leeds, because any meeting with those rebel clubs would lead to expulsion. It was a high price to pay and no club was going to take any risks lightly. Crumbie had to get busy and find adequate replacements if at all possible.

As the 1895–96 season got underway, the Tigers, resplendent in their new scarlet, green and white hooped shirts, which were first worn on 25 September 1895, experienced a turnover of players from the northern counties in their first team. Bob Hesmondhalgh, for whatever reason, played his last regular game for the Tigers at the start of December 1895 aged just 26, although he played one more match in November 1898.

Among the new recruits was William Yiend, aged 35 and formerly with Hartlepool Rovers, who made his debut on 19 October. A former England forward, who won six caps between 1889 and 1893, Yiend was a non-contentious recruit because he had moved to work as a railway traffic agent in Peterborough. Yiend only spent one season with the Tigers before retiring, after which he remained active as a very capable referee.

There was more concern about another couple of recruits. The Tigers recruited a forward, Robert Campbell, who was born in 1875, formerly with Morecambe, who made his debut on 21 September and a half-back,

Jackie Braithwaite, formerly with Holbeck, who made his debut on 12 October. Braithwaite was an engineer by trade. Both their former clubs, Holbeck and Morecambe, would join the NU in spring 1896.

Rugby Union in Leicestershire was controlled by the Midland Counties Union, a body that was led by a core group of hard-line amateurs based around Birmingham. Following the Midland Counties versus Middlesex match, held at Rugby, on Wednesday 13 November 1895, the Midlands' full-back, Alf Butlin, of Rugby FC, approached a group of Leicester officials and asked to join the Tigers. Those officials present encouraged him and Butlin was included in the Tigers' team, as a winger, for the match against Swinton on Saturday 23 November. Butlin was employed an engine cleaner and lived in Rugby.

On the morning of the match Arnold Crane, the Midland Counties secretary, declared Butlin ineligible. As Leicester departed for Manchester on the 8.25am train, Crumbie did not receive the letter in time to prevent Butlin making his debut on the wing. It was hardly an auspicious introduction to the team because Swinton beat Leicester 13-0. Crane sent an account of the events to the RFU and although he made no specific charges an inquiry was ordered. It was assumed that Rugby FC had instigated the action.

An inquiry was held by the Midland Counties committee at the Great Western Hotel, Birmingham on Tuesday 17 December. Once proceedings were underway it became clear that Crane had based his actions on the transfer rules that had applied for 1894–95. Crumbie was aware of that and focused Leicester's defence on that point – that a new set of transfer rules were in force for 1895–96 and so the prosecution's case fell. The basis for Crane's decision to bar Butlin from playing was false and the inquiry unanimously granted his transfer. Rugby FC was held responsible for the inquiry and had to bear the costs of the proceedings, much to the astonishment of their officials.

With that Butlin was able, once again, to take his place in the Tigers' line-up at Northampton on Saturday 21 December. The Tigers were well served at full-back by Arthur Jones, who was club captain from 1896 to 1899, and Butlin had to play in the threequarters until mid-1897.

The end of the inquiry did not close the matter. A meeting of the RFU's professionalism sub-committee was held at Rugby on 19 February 1896. Its three members – W. Cail (Northumberland), J.A. Miller (Yorkshire) and G.F. Berney (Surrey) – met to investigate accusations of inducements offered by Leicester to players. After sitting for over three hours the sub-committee decided that 1) there were no problems associated with Butlin's transfer; 2) that in bringing the charge Rugby FC had acted in the best interests of the game and 3) ordered Midland Counties Union to pay the costs of the first inquiry.

William Cail said afterwards there had been several suspicious cases involving Leicester – first Foreman and then Redman – and it was because of those cases the enquiry had been held. Leicester had a bad name for poaching and using undue influence. But, they had come out of the enquiry clean and he hoped in future they would be more circumspect. On behalf of the club committee, John Parsons, the Leicester president, said they were pleased to have put their books and evidence before the committee. In a letter to the *Leicester Daily Mercury* one correspondent said that the whole affair should act as a spur to the club committee to throw "in their lot with the Northern Union, which would furnish a greater attraction and better football for their supporters."

It is not known what were Crumbie's contingency plans in the event of the enquiry's decision going against the Tigers, but according to some sources they had entered into discussions with the NU in case they were expelled by the RFU.

While the Tigers' management could point to their team's home-grown talent, like Sid Penny, who made his debut on 4 January 1896, in their defence, they immediately took advantage of the Butlin verdict to invite another of Rugby FC's players, W.F. Lincoln, a forward, to join them on their Easter tour. Lincoln accepted, played against Hartlepool Rovers on 18 April 1896, and switched clubs for the following season.

However, the Tiger's ambitions still propelled the committee to search for recruits outside the midlands. During 1896–97, Erving Mosby, a wing or centre who hailed from Normanton in west Yorkshire, made a couple of appearances in the Leicester first team. He made his debut on 15 December 1896. It was obviously to his liking because Mosby threw in his lot with the Tigers for 1897–98. His former home town club, Normanton, joined the NU in May 1898.

The Northern Union restructures

News from the north was confusing. As its first season drew to a close the NU committee dealt with the issue of its future competition structure at a meeting on 5 March 1896. Realising that the Northern Rugby League was placing too high a demand on its members, with 42 fixtures, and aware that a new group of prospective members were in the process of preparing applications the Committee decided that the senior clubs would be split into two county based leagues – the

133

Lancashire and Yorkshire Senior Competitions – with either 26 or 30 fixtures respectively in 1896–97. This arrangement would operate for the next five seasons.

After their run in with the RFU three weeks earlier, the Tigers, one of the few clubs in the midlands with the gate receipts to follow the lead of the northern rebels, were offered few options by the NU's re-organisation. They could form a Midlands competition and affiliate that to the NU, or apply to join either of the existing senior competitions.

There was insufficient local support for the former and it was very unlikely due to demand for places that Leicester would be accepted by the latter. Even if the latter option, which would see the Tigers lose most of their local fixtures, was a possibility it would hardly guarantee good receipts unless all the visiting clubs could draw a gate.

As the Tigers' had enemies, Crumbie had to be very careful how he conducted the club's affairs. Recognising his lack of viable options Crumbie appears to have concentrated on maintaining the Tigers' financial strength and therefore some degree of independence within the RFU. A further shift came in July 1898 when the NU allowed professionalism under strict conditions – thereby losing the support of any amateurs they had – and not necessarily gaining the support of anyone who favoured open professionalism. It was another shift in attitude that did not necessarily appeal outside Yorkshire and Lancashire. The rule gave the founding members almost complete control of the NU was not one that would have appealed to Crumbie.

Crumbie had assumed secretarial – effectively managerial – responsibility at a club that had big ambitions, but narrower fixture options than before. To help fill the ground the Tigers had started to organise a Christmas Festival each year, and invited clubs to participate in what was usually a programme of three games over four days or sometimes four games over five days.

Prior to Crumbie's appointment the Tigers' management had tendency to look north for new and better fixtures. Some northern opponents, particularly from the Manchester area such as Broughton Rangers, Salford and Swinton, had found their way onto the Tigers' list. However, there were big questions about the long term future of those fixtures and even the likely replacements such as Altrincham.

Leicester also had strained relations with Moseley, one of its most senior neighbours. Passions had run so high in the Midland Counties Cup semi-final at The Reddings on 23 March 1895 that Moseley refused to arrange any regular fixtures with the Tigers for the next eight seasons. Moseley did, however, fulfil Midland Counties Cup ties between the clubs that seemed to arise on an almost annual basis during that period. Another local rival, Rugby FC, had become so weak that it dropped first team fixtures with the Tigers for two seasons.

Fortunately, an intense and generally friendly rivalry was developing with Northampton, a keen rugby playing town 30 miles to the south. A visit by Northampton's Saints to Welford Road on 6 November 1897 drew a crowd of 12,000. There were no other midlands' clubs capable of drawing that kind of attendance.

As a result of clubs joining the NU, disbanding in a few cases or simply being unable to find the money to travel long distances, fixture lists across the country suffered major disruption for a number of years. Crumbie was fortunate that the Tigers' funds were sufficiently healthy for him to go in search for new crowd-pleasing opponents in areas of the country to the south and west that presented some travel problems.

His first targets were in the south west of England – the Tigers travelled there and played Devonport Albion and Bridgwater in April 1896. Fixtures with some small Welsh clubs, such as Penygraig, Cardiff Harlequins and Pontypridd, had been played before 1895, but what Crumbie needed was the big names.

There was a question mark hanging over the longevity of any arrangements with Welsh clubs once the arguments over the A.J. Gould affair began in January 1896. A significant section of the RFU wanted to deal firmly with the Welsh Union over Gould. They also harboured suspicions about the amateur credentials of its leading clubs. If that lead to a new split in the game so be it as far as they were concerned. That did not deter the Tigers and a short tour to south Wales in October 1896 produced matches against Llanelli, Mountain Ash and Swansea. The Tigers were able to welcome return visits from both Swansea, at the start of February 1897, and Llanelli, two months later, for the first time.

There was a real prospect in the summer of 1897 that cross border club matches would be banned. If the amateur purists had gained control of the RFU there was a strong possibility of a new split that would have seen the west of England clubs as the focus of a new breakaway body.

That possibility receded as a result of the vote at the 16 September 1897 RFU AGM when the committee was defeated by a large majority on the issue of clubs being able to play matches against teams including Gould. One of the motivations behind that vote was that if the motion in question was not passed it would put a severe strain on the loyalties of those English clubs anxious for Welsh fixtures. However, *The Sporting Life* was concerned that the longer the impasse over international matches continued the more likely it became that the WFU would approve the formation of a national league. If that happened it would reduce the possibility of fixtures with leading clubs in the west country and the midlands, thus directly reducing their income.

At a time of tension Crumbie saw his opportunity. In addition to south Wales, Crumbie managed to secure fixtures with Bristol – at the time the focus for the opposition to the RFU's stance over Gould – for 1897–98. By the time the Gould affair drew to a close in April 1898, Crumbie had reached agreement for home and away fixtures with Cardiff for 1898–99 and finally secured a similar arrangement with Gould's club, Newport, in 1900–01. The Tigers were not particularly successful on tour – they recorded only two victories in south Wales, over Treherbert in 1898–99 and Llanelli in 1900–01 in the first 20 years of these matches. Leicester had lost some of their northern opponents who had joined the NU, but were now playing some of the leading clubs from Wales.

'Friendlies' provided the bulk of the Tigers' fixture list; the only competitive matches included each season were the rounds of the Midland Counties Cup. Winning that trophy, which had predominantly been in the hands of clubs from the west of the region, became the Tigers' main goal. Assembling a winning team was not the Tigers' only problem; Welford Road's appalling pitch nearly caused the club to be turfed out of the competition for 1897–98.

Fresh turf, at a cost of £500, not only kept the Tigers in the Cup, it spurred them on to win the trophy for the first time. The Tigers were so determined to win that when the Cup Final was postponed to accommodate the final of the County Championship, also arranged for The Butts at Coventry, all their players withdrew from the Midland Counties team that was due to face Northumberland. Without the Tigers' contingent the Midland Counties could make no impression and lost 24–3. Ten days later, on Wednesday 6 April 1898, the full strength Tigers, having achieved a narrow victory over Moseley, returned home to be met by thousands of their supporters who lined the streets all the way from the LMS railway station, along Granby Street, to the club's headquarters, the George Hotel, by the clock tower.

That victory marked the start of an eight year spell in which the trophy remained in the Tigers' hands, which showed how expertly their team had been assembled. Even though Erving Mosby did not play, the Tigers' team at the Butts included five of the most high profile imports – Alf Butlin, Billy Foreman, John Braithwaite, Edward Redman and Robert Campbell – alongside a couple of recruits from nearer home – Percy

Atkins and Frank Jones, both Bedford School products – who had played for Nuneaton. There could have been a third former Nuneaton player in the team, but J.W. 'Sid' Matthews, who had made his debut in January 1898, was not selected. Home grown players such as M.E. Whitehead, John Garner, Arthur Akers, Sid Penny and Walter Jackson provided the majority of the pack.

Yet such were the amateur constraints placed on team building, it ought to have been expected that such a style of team building would become much more difficult and force Leicester to be ever more reliant on locally developed talent. And locally based talent was coming through from all sections of the community. A young winger, educated at Uppingham, Alfred Hind, made his debut in October 1899 and went on to win a Blue at Cambridge in 1900.

Crumbie obviously had his own views about how the club and team development should be handled. When he took over as secretary the Tigers were fielding three teams every week, but around the turn of the century he decided to disband the 'B' team.

The Northern Rugby League

Dissatisfaction at the Northern Union's league structure led a number of leading clubs to form a new Northern Rugby League. It was a controversial move, but finally the new competition with 14 members gained official recognition at the start of June 1901. Even before it was recognised the organisers, in a bid to increase the new league's standing, had invited Leicester, as the Midland Counties Cup holders, to join.

Being champions of the midlands gave the Tigers some standing, but how well would they match up to the fully professional members of the League? What would it cost to strengthen the team and build a professional infrastructure within the club to meet the challenge? Was such a risky proposition worth jeopardising all that had been achieved over the last five years? How committed were the club members and supporters to amateurism and the RFU? Would the Tigers' committee be prepared to try and convince their fans of the NRL's potential and turn their backs on friendly fixtures?

It was felt by many that it was likely that the Tigers' committee would take the least risky and most commercially advantageous options available to them. A journalist writing in *The Yorkshire Post* on 22 May 1901 summed up the position well when he wrote that the Tigers had been "extensively patronised by the English Rugby Union, as well as by the crack southern clubs, and really do not need any attraction in the way of the Northern Union". As the writer anticipated Leicester shunned the approach and stayed loyal to the RFU.

It was a decision that paid off as other leading southern clubs – London Welsh (1902–03), Oxford University (1903–04) and London Scottish (1904–05) – joined Richmond (1898–99) and Cambridge University (1899–00) as regulars on the Tigers' fixture list. To make space certain less prestigious neighbouring clubs such as Burton, Handsworth and Nuneaton were dropped from the fixture list. The strengthening of the fixture list proved popular with the Tigers' supporters and Crumbie never missed an opportunity to widen the club's ambitions.

Following revision by the English and Welsh Unions, a new draft of the professional laws was approved in October 1901 and almost immediately caused Leicester, and many of their midland neighbours, problems. On the day of the Tigers' visit to Franklin's Gardens, Saturday 23 November 1901, news broke that Northampton Saints' highly rated half-back, Billy Patrick, had been approached by NU scouts and had signed a form for Bradford a couple of weeks earlier since when he appeared against Lennox and for East Midlands against Kent. Merely signing a NU form had not been a professional offence prior to the new draft being approved and Patrick seemed unaware of the implications of his action. He was immediately declared a professional, but by appearing that day against Leicester he had, as a correspondent pointed out in the local press, technically professionalised both his team mates and his opponents. It was widely expected that Patrick would make his debut for Bradford in a friendly against Hull KR the following Saturday, but he did not and in fact never played in the NU.

The decision not to strictly apply the new law to those who took the field alongside Patrick exposed its limitations, but did not bring about its repeal. If it had been enforced the Tigers would have lost an entire first team as would a number of other clubs over the next few years.

The Tigers' arch rivals Northampton had had problems with northern recruiters – Sam Williams and Charlie Civil had joined Oldham in 1897 and 1901 respectively before Patrick's defection. However, very few of Leicester's players were attracted by offers to 'go north'.

When Edward Redman returned to Yorkshire in 1898–99 he joined Keighley, a club agonising over whether or not to resign from the RFU. Although nearing the veteran stage, Redman's play was still well enough regarded and he won his 13th Yorkshire cap against Cheshire on 20 January 1900. Redman chose not to follow Keighley into the NU when they finally made the switch in April 1900, which allowed him to make a farewell appearance for the Tigers on 5 November 1900.

Erving Mosby severed his connections with the Tigers and joined Bradford in the new Northern Rugby League in July 1901. By the time he made his last appearance for the Tigers on 23 March 1901 Mosby had played 73 times for Leicester. Mosby played for Bradford until 1907–08, during which time he appeared for Yorkshire and played for England against Other Nationalities at Park Avenue in January 1905.

Billy Foreman also let it be known that he had been approached on several occasions by NU clubs, but had rejected them all. According to Foreman this was because of "the good feelings that existed between himself, the committee and the people of the town." In January 1903 a Leicester centre, R.W. Dakin, was erroneously thought to be on the verge of agreeing terms with Hunslet. However, when Mr Biggins, the Hunslet treasurer, arrived in Leicester on 24 January to obtain his signature he was kidnapped by a group of Tigers who forced him to stand a round of whisky and cigars and send a telegram to Hunslet stating that he had "fallen into... the tiger's claws". Having paid, Biggins, who apparently took it all in good part, was allowed to return home, needless to say without Dakin's signature. Two years later Dakin moved on to Coventry RUFC.

As the position of rugby union in Yorkshire became increasingly desperate some leading players switched allegiance to Leicester. One of the first to move south was S. Neuman who joined the Tigers after his club, Cleckheaton, joined the NU in 1900. He captained Yorkshire in 1900–01, and played 22 times for the Tigers that season. He played his last match for the Tigers at the start of November 1901. Ernest Walton, who was educated at St Peters, York and Oxford University, won four England caps at half-back in 1900–01 and 1901–02 while with Castleford. He made one appearance for the Tigers on 28 September 1901 before taking employment in India. Richard Russell who had been educated at St Peters, York and Cambridge University, won 13 Yorkshire caps between 1899–00 and 1901–02 while playing for Castleford. He made his debut for Leicester in September 1903.

Welford Road

The Tigers were a genuinely popular institution in the town. Gates were good and the committee was keen to improve them. Leicester's membership at the end of the nineteenth century was around 1,200. To further increase support the club offered a cheap 3/- (£0.15) season ticket which gave access to the less popular sides of the ground.

The Tigers' ground was on land leased from Leicester Council. After an investment of £1,300 to re-position the members stand, which ran along the touchline on the north side of the pitch, Welford Road's capacity stood at 19,800 in 1899, with seats for 3,000. It was becoming a worthy home for the Midland champions, and was far larger than many rugby union club grounds were in the 1990s before the game went 'open', let alone at this time. The capacity was needed for Leicester's supporters would turn out in the large numbers, over 10,000, for matches against local rivals, such as Northampton, and for the visits of Welsh clubs like Swansea.

Having turned its back on all its major northern venues, the RFU desperately needed other provincial grounds for its international matches and Welford Road was an obvious prospect. It was chosen to host the North versus South trial match on 24 February 1900. 'Sid' Matthews played for the South. This was the first time a much of such importance had been played in the Midland Counties. Although bad weather kept the attendance below expectations a greater honour soon followed when the RFU assigned the England versus Ireland match to Welford Road and it was held there on 8 February 1902. Although no Leicester players were selected the cancellation of all junior matches on that day helped to draw a crowd estimated at 14,000. Pleased with the response the RFU staged the England versus Wales match there on 9 January 1904.

Recognition for the ground brought in its wake recognition for some of those who regularly played upon it. The first was John Miles, a former pupil at Medway Street School who, at Swansea on 10 January 1903, became the first player to win an England cap direct from the club. Miles was followed into the England team the following year by a product of Oakham School and Cambridge University, George Keeton. Although he did play for Leicester, Keeton, who won the first of his three caps against Wales on 9 January 1904 at Welford Road, was seen more regularly in Richmond's colours.

The County Union

The Tigers weren't just focused on achieving their own targets. In March 1901 the Leicestershire Union wrote to the Tigers to draw their attention to the need for efforts to be made to start new clubs in different parts of the county. Support was forthcoming and on 25 September 1901 the two bodies agreed to combine under the auspices of the County Union to further the game's interest by promoting exhibitions and lobbying the local authorities for pitches. The combined body ran until December 1902.

In 1902 Fred Toone resigned after five years as secretary of the Leicestershire RFU, a position he held at the same time as being secretary of Leicestershire CCC; Toone had been appointed secretary of the Yorkshire CCC. He was succeeded by Sydney Packer, a local coal merchant, who held the office until 1919.

Packer pushed the introduction of a scheme for an insurance fund that covered the local junior clubs. He convinced Crumbie of its value and Leicester Tigers became guarantors of the scheme. Crumbie also made an initial donation of £20 so the fund could begin on 1 January 1903. The Tigers also made grants on an annual basis to the district's junior clubs. Welford Road regularly provided a stage for the district's leading junior clubs. Although prevented from mounting a first team challenge, the Tigers regularly hosted two local cup finals – the County Senior Cup, which began in 1890, and the Rolleston Charity Cup competition, which began in 1896 – each spring. Sir John Rolleston was President of the Leicestershire RFU from 1896 to 1910.

The Schools' Union

In addition to hosting high profile representative matches, Leicester FC found time to be very supportive of the Leicester Schools Football League (Rugby Union), later the Leicester and District Schools RFU, which had been formed in August 1894. Welford Road was made available for major school matches, and the club granted £3 and 18 season tickets to each competing school every season. Such was the enthusiasm for the game in the town that the Union, which catered for under-14s, had enough elementary schools in membership to run two divisions in their league competition.

The Union's honorary secretary, J.C. Cooper, a teacher at Medway Street School, also played a major role in the launch of the English Schools RFU, which was formed at the Leicester YMCA on 26 March 1904. The first schools international in England was held at Welford Road in March 1905 and drew a crowd of 5,000. That attendance was more than enough to ensure that Welford Road became the regular venue for the bi-annual match against the Welsh schools up to the First World War.

The club's strength is shown through the Midlands County Cup results:

Midland Counties Cup Finals
6 April 1898   Leicester 5 Moseley 3   Coventry
1 April 1899   Leicester 20 Nuneaton 3   Coventry

31 March 1900	Leicester 13 Moseley 4	Coventry
30 March 1901	Leicester 8 Moseley 3	Rugby
29 March 1902	Leicester 5 Moseley 0	Coventry
4 April 1903	Leicester 18 Rugby 0	Coventry
2 April 1904	Leicester 13 Moseley 3	Burton
1 April 1905	Leicester 31 Nottingham 0	Coventry

In 1901, besides Mosby a number of other regular first-teamers had left the club. Robert Campbell had played his last match for the Tigers in September 1901, aged only 26. Alf Butlin would play his last match for the Tigers at Northampton on 13 December 1902. It was Butlin's 252nd appearance for the Tigers. As those long-serving players moved on, Crumbie acted to find new recruits to maintain the Tigers' standing.

The start of the Cornish connection – the Jacketts

Ten years earlier, Leicester had looked northwards for new recruits, but in 1904 a new region, the south west, emerged as a source of players. John Jackett first appeared at full-back for Leicester on 29 December 1904. He was 22 years old and had spent some time serving with the mounted police in Transvaal. Jackett had played rugby union during his time in South Africa and had been included in a Transvaal XV that met the 1903 British Isles touring team.

After an interval of nearly three years, he had last played for Cornwall against Devon on 17 November 1900, Jackett regained his place in the Cornwall team to face Somerset on 31 October 1903. Jackett's play in that and the next two county matches must have impressed for he was appointed captain of Cornwall in 1904–05. He had appeared as captain three times when he made his debut for Leicester. Although he would continue to be referred to as a member of the Falmouth club Jackett appeared very regularly for the Tigers from then onwards. It was the start of a short-lived, but significant Cornish connection for the club.

John's brother Richard, a very strong, hard-working forward, having entered senior rugby with Falmouth had also secured a regular place in the Cornwall XV in 1901–02. Richard also received invitations from Leicester and appeared on 59 occasions for the Tigers after making his debut in April 1905.

1905 to 1909: On Crumbie's invitation

In the summer of 1904 an official tour of Europe by a party of New Zealand rugby footballers in 1905–06 was confirmed. To meet the tour's

142

projected costs it was agreed that each opponent would be required to make a guarantee, ranging up to £500 for an international match, against 70 per cent of the gate receipts. Leicester was one of 10 English clubs sufficiently popular to be confident that their gate receipts would meet the guarantee required for a match. It was a mark of Leicester's standing that they were one of only three clubs – the others were Blackheath and Richmond – that felt able to book a Saturday fixture.

The Tigers had enjoyed an unbeaten start to the season and were expected to provide strong opposition for the tourists in their fifth match. To better appreciate the size of the task facing them the Tigers travelled to Northampton on Thursday 28 September 1905. To try and match the tourists Northampton had brought in four guests – two from Civil Service and two from London Hospitals. The Tigers' players were part of a 6,500 strong crowd that could only watch in awe as the recently christened All Blacks demolished the Saints 32–0. It's not clear whether the Tigers' party that journeyed to Northampton included a new recruit, Fred Jackson, who was scheduled to make his debut against the All Blacks at Welford Road.

Leicester's supporters turned out in force to produce a new ground record attendance, estimated at 16,000, with receipts of £392, three days later. This was the second highest attendance achieved by an English club – later in the tour Devonport Albion welcomed over 19,000. The much vaunted Tigers proved no match for the New Zealanders, and conceded six tries in a 28-0 defeat. Speaking at the post-match dinner Dave Gallaher, the All Blacks' skipper, complimented his hosts on their performance: "When we were down south we were told that when we got to Leicester we should know about it. Well we do know about it. You gave us one of the hardest games I have ever played in." It was a compliment that was not shared by another journalist, who, after watching the match, concluded in *The Referee* that "… there is something rotten in the state of English Rugby Football."

As the victories mounted interest in the tourists just kept growing. By the time the All Blacks returned to Leicester to meet the Midland Counties on 28 October, demand to see them was huge. Special trains had been laid on from many parts of the midlands and all stand seats were sold out well beforehand. On the day it was estimated that over 19,000 crammed into the ground, which produced receipts of over £700. Although the Midland Counties XV, including seven Tigers – Alfred Hind, John Braithwaite, 'Sid' Matthews, Richard Russell, Percy Atkins, Dudley Atkins and Alf Goodrich – was no match for the All Blacks, the huge crowd at least saw the tourists concede only their second try in 13 matches.

Four Leicester players had impressed the selectors sufficiently to make their England debuts against the All Blacks on Saturday 2 December 1905. The Tigers appearing for England that day were two former public schoolboys, Alfred Hind and Richard Russell, the long-standing Yorkshire import, Jackie Braithwaite, and at full-back, John Jackett who had appeared for Cornwall against New Zealand.

Having been trounced by the All Blacks, the Tigers briefly tried to emulate them by adopting their team formation – eight backs and seven forwards – against some opponents in 1905–06 and 1906–07. For those matches the team had to be restructured and Percy Atkins was pressed into service as a rover wing-forward. It was a time of change as two key figures, the long-serving half backs – Jackie Braithwaite and Billy Foreman – retired in December and February 1906 respectively – although Foreman had not been a regular in the team since summer 1904.

Alfred Hind and John Jackett retained their places in the England team that met Wales on 13 January at Richmond. Only Jackett kept his place for the England versus Ireland match at Welford Road on 10 February 1906, when the attendance was a relatively disappointing 10,000.

Overall, the season's receipts had been much greater than ever before which left the Tigers' coffers full of cash. If it so wished, the club could afford to be generous. When Leicester had an unexpected fixture vacancy on 10 March 1906, Crumbie arranged to fill it with a first visit from Headingley. Crumbie guaranteed the visitor's travelling expenses of £25. The fixture became an annual one.

With the Tigers obtaining guarantees to cover the cost of the Easter tour's travel, meals and accommodation for the full five days, all the player had to cover was his drinks, tobacco and any other domestic out-of-pocket expenses. It is hardly surprising those tours proved popular, especially with players whose own clubs lacked the resources to organise something similar.

John Jackett and Fred Jackson had made a major contribution to the Tigers' first team over 1905–06 – making 23 appearances each by the time it came to the end of season Easter tour. Both went on tour where they were joined by two forwards from the north-east of England. Alfred Kewney of Rockcliff had made his debut in the England pack against Wales on 13 January 1906 and held his place for the rest of the season. For England's final match of the season, against France on 22 March, Kewney was joined in the pack by Tom Hogarth of Hartlepool Rovers, who was making his debut. Subsequently both men were invited to join Leicester's Easter tour; Hartlepool Rovers gave permission for Hogarth to take part. Both made their debuts for the Tigers against Newport on

Easter Saturday, 14 April, 1906. Two more matches, against Cardiff on Easter Monday and Bristol the next day, completed that Easter's itinerary.

Yet there were signs of internal dissent. Within the club there seem to have been some who harboured doubts about the direction Crumbie was taking. The most notable was probably Alfred Hind. Hind was the club's vice-captain, but he resigned at the end of January 1906, only a couple of weeks after winning his second England cap, and joined Nottingham.

There was a major difference as the season drew to a close. There was no triumphant return to the town with the Midland Counties Cup. Leicester had withdrawn after eight consecutive victories to give other, weaker, clubs a chance of winning.

Within Leicester's newer suburbs there were a number of smaller rugby clubs with good playing reputations. While those smaller clubs – such as Belgrave and Stoneygate – were denied regular first team fixtures with the Tigers, they did manage to exchange fixtures with the first teams of some other leading midlands clubs. Those smaller clubs were also members of the Midland Counties Union and were able to enter its cup competition, which provided a reasonable chance of a meeting with the Tigers. Such meetings generally were a mismatch – as Belgrave discovered the hard way in 1903 when the Tigers routed them, 54-0. During the Tigers' absence from the Midland Counties Cup, Stoneygate did its bit for the town's honour by reaching the semi-final in 1906, where they lost to the eventual winners, Nottingham.

The Tigers regarded the smaller clubs as a source of talent and regularly recruited from them. However, recruitment of players, especially for the Tigers' 'A' team, was a constant source of friction. Stoneygate may have been proud that John Miles, a former member, had won his first England cap as a Tiger, but they felt sufficiently aggrieved to feel it necessary to write to Crumbie complaining about calls on their players in 1903. Miles's playing career with Leicester ended in April 1904 because of increasing business commitments. When those commitments proved to be less onerous than he expected, Miles chose to join Northampton in November 1904.

There had obviously been plenty of discussions about a future direction prior to the Leicestershire Rugby Union AGM in July 1906. There Crumbie proposed that Leicester FC take control of the junior league, formed in June 1897. He endorsed the scheme, saying that "a number of senior clubs would be formed into a competition with Leicester 'A' under certain obligations whereby players should be drafted into the 'A' team which should be considered a stepping stone to the premier team."

145

Syd Packer's report to the AGM included his own committee's commitment to the scheme: "We must cultivate our own produce and no better scheme has been formulated whereby the best talents can play together. We hope to make Leicester 'A', the strongest 'A' team in the country, as it is our desire to make the Leicester First XV pre-eminent. This of course lies with our local lads and it is felt that they will, now the opportunity has been given, show of what quality they are made."

Agreement for this new initiative was forthcoming on 29 August from the Leicestershire Rugby Union. The competition was renamed the Leicester Football Club Alliance and it was intended that it would comprise the eight clubs previously in membership of the junior league plus Leicester 'A'. The Alliance plan was subsequently endorsed by the Midland Counties Union, although some individuals harboured doubts about the efficacy of dual control, by the County and the Tigers, of the same clubs. It was expected that the new arrangement would advance junior rugby in the district and help prepare players for promotion to the Tigers' first team. Everyone agreed it was, if successful, an arrangement that would promote local player development.

Just when everything appeared settled a new problem arose. When the Tigers were unable to field an 'A' team for the opening match of the new season at Oadby, a situation that was blamed on the lack of support from other Alliance members, Crumbie surprisingly announced that the 'A' team, which had enjoyed some success in the Midlands Junior Cup, was disbanded. At a stroke those players who were the core of the 'A' team had no choice but to leave the club if they wished to continue playing regularly. There was one small positive outcome – at least from then onwards the members of the Alliance would only be expected to release players to the Tigers' first team whenever the need arose.

That agreement effectively formalised the position whereby members of the Alliance had been demoted to the role of feeder teams. That demotion and the ill-feeling that grew out of last minute demands from Welford Road for players led to bad relations for many years. That resentment may well have been the reason that Crumbie was one of the people summarily removed from the list of vice presidents at the next County Rugby Union AGM in September 1907.

There was another reason for dispensing with the 'A' team – it served no purpose once Crumbie had decided that Leicester would in future be run as an invitation club. Most of those invited by the Tigers' selection committee would be players with local clubs and draw little attention.

146

However, a number of leading players from across the country also received invites to play for the club.

That decision meant that Leicester would no longer function as an open members' club. No subscriptions or entry fee would be payable. The responsibility for ensuring a team of sufficient quality was fielded for each match fell inevitably on Crumbie's shoulders. The responsibility for covering the cost of Crumbie's efforts was shouldered by F. St Clair Pain, the treasurer of the Tigers, who was elected to that office in 1904 and would hold it for the next 15 years.

Although Crumbie could field attractive teams at Welford Road and on tour there was criticism that the club failed to field strong sides for some Saturday away matches. There was also the problem that bedevils all invitation sides to be faced – that no matter how good the individuals, the resultant team will struggle to overcome settled quality opposition.

Nursery clubs

Being a nursery club was a role Stoneygate performed well. Stoneygate's annual membership fee was increased to 10 shillings in 1904. As members of the Alliance, players from Stoneygate continued to graduate into the Leicester first XV. One of the first was Kenneth Wood, a centre, who made his debut in October 1906. By 1908 Wood was part of a group of eight former Stoneygate members in the Tigers' ranks. Both Stoneygate and another Alliance member, Westleigh, which had been formed as a split off from Stoneygate in 1904 played on the municipally owned Victoria Park for a weekly fee. Both clubs, having accepted the role of nursery, were only too happy after 1908 to be invited to meet each other at Welford Road every November, the gate receipts being shared for their own funds. It was difficult for an ambitious junior club to rise and prosper when the Tigers' largesse made up a significant proportion of their income.

The first Springboks

In the footsteps of the All Blacks there followed the first Springboks. Such was the demand for fixtures that clubs were excluded, in favour of representative sides, from this and all future major tour itineraries. For the second match of their tour the Springboks drew nearly 14,000 spectators, with receipts of £500, to Welford Road on Saturday 29 September 1906, a figure only slightly down on the equivalent fixture with the Midland Counties the previous year. A Midland Counties XV

147

containing seven Tigers – James Bainbridge, John Braithwaite, Richard Russell, Sid Penny, Sid Matthews, Alf Goodrich and Percy Atkins – was outclassed, and lost 29–0.

A new interest in recruitment raised some eyebrows. The most emotion was generated by the switch of A.J. Hobbs, who had apparently severed his links with Northampton, after over 100 appearances for that club, to pursue business interests in Leicester. Hobbs's appearance in the Tigers' pack on 8 September 1906 led the fixture secretary of his former club to write to *The Birmingham Post* accusing Leicester of poaching.

The loss of Hobbs was compounded when an unemployed Frank Coles took a job in Leicester and joined the Tigers. Coles made two appearances as a centre for the Tigers in September 1906 before he decided to return to Northampton – apparently because his bride to be would not relocate. Others had a different interpretation.

Veiled professionalism

Enough events seemed to have occurred to convince the pristine amateurs that something untoward was happening in the midlands and possibly elsewhere. Following wide ranging accusations of veiled professionalism made by Percy Adams, the president of the Birmingham based Old Edwardians, the RFU committee established a commission to look at the problem on 6 December 1906. It comprised W. Cail (Northumberland), C.A. Crane (Midlands), W.S. Donne (Somerset), J. Baxter (Cheshire) and F. Waters (Surrey). It was to conduct an investigation nationally and collect evidence of malpractice where appropriate. Having to establish the commission at this time was hardly good news coming as it did when the committee had an outside chance of recruiting some former leading members from the NU.

The investigation into veiled professionalism moved at a leisurely pace around the country. Finally three members of the commission – Baxter, Cail and Waters – arrived at the Grand Hotel, Leicester, to conduct interviews on Tuesday 17 December 1907. Once installed there the commission, with the assistance of Adams and J.F. Byrne (the honorary secretary of Moseley), interviewed representatives of the Coventry, Leicester and Northampton clubs over three separate days. Both Leicester and Northampton were questioned regarding Frank Coles's switch of clubs. Their answers were accepted and it appeared that the Tigers had no charges to answer. However, Northampton was told to change its after match hospitality. In future the players should be restricted to tea and not tea and cigarettes as previously offered. Although players with both Leicester and Northampton were instructed to refund payments received from their clubs no evidence of veiled professionalism was found anywhere.

The RFU received the commission's report on Monday 2 March 1908. It found no evidence of veiled professionalism, but did say that there had been evidence of too lavish expenditure on entertainment, provided in order to attract players, and irregularities in some club books. Among the latter it found problems with clubs not keeping separate insurance funds, having funds properly audited, showing sufficient detail on club balance sheets, paying players' expenses without having details and providing unnecessary refreshment

The report was viewed sceptically by some leading figures in the Midlands who considered the commission had pursued its task half-heartedly.

By coincidence it was also a time when the Tigers once again had some public contact with the activities of NU scouts. For a change those scouts enjoyed some success and two threequarters, Fred Hardyman, who made 39 appearances for the Tigers between his debut at Plymouth on 9 October 1905 and his farewell appearance on 20 April 1907, and J. Jackson who made his debut on 27 November 1906[†] joined Broughton Rangers, and made their debuts in September 1907. Also, a half-back, T.W. Wilson, who made five appearances for the Tigers starting in April 1907, signed for Leeds in the 1907–08 season.

A visit by Swansea was always a draw – even when the Tigers' successful association football neighbours Leicester Fosse were playing at home in a Division Two match against Clapton Orient on Saturday 16 February 1907, the attendance at Welford Road was reported as 9,000. By comparison Bradford, 15 years earlier one of the strongest clubs in the land, was facing up to significant losses because of the challenge from Bradford City, like Fosse also members of Division Two. So bad had things become, the average attendance at Park Avenue was only just over 4,000, that Bradford's committee was considering resigning from the NU and rejoining the RFU.

The Tigers' comparative affluence must have been one of the reasons that some leading NU clubs were considering being lured back into membership of the RFU. The Tigers' operations were probably the model for any reconstituted club, like Bradford, to adopt if it accepted

---

[†] This may have been the Tom Jackson who had made 36 appearances for the Tigers since 1904.

149

the RFU's offer to rejoin, made in mid-March, and a fixture with Leicester would have been a major incentive for it to take the plunge.

Perhaps by coincidence the Tigers included few high-profile invitees while the commission on professionalism was on the prowl in 1906–07. Or maybe the terrible weather, which forced the cancellation of all three matches on the New Year tour to the north-east as well as the Boxing Day visit by Birkenhead Park and the home matches against Moseley and Cardiff, meant that there was not the money available to fund guests at Easter.

Whatever the reason, almost immediately after the investigating committee had visited Leicester and given the club a clean bill of health, things changed. Although he was never an outlaw at heart, Crumbie was always an oppositionist and he seems to have seized upon that outcome to ramp up the invitation policy. It was a strange decision because Charles Crane assumed the Presidency of the RFU at the AGM held on 30 May 1907. Crane, who lived in Pershore in Worcestershire, had spent an unprecedented five years as senior vice-president, patiently waiting for his turn to become president and put into practice his vision of the game's future. It was well known, from his activities in the midlands, that he was no friend of the Tigers.

Leicester's New Year tour of 1908 included only two matches – a meeting with West Hartlepool on 1 January and with neighbouring Rovers the following day. The Tigers' party that set off for Hartlepool had a distinctly Celtic feel to it. A Welsh international full-back, John Dyke of Penarth, was included in the party. In addition to the two Cornish regulars – Fred Jackson and John Jackett – the party included the latter's brother, Richard, James 'Maffer' Davey and 'Dicky' Eathorne. 'Maffer' Davey of Redruth, a stand-off, had returned to Cornwall the previous summer after spending six years working in the gold mines of South Africa and was now a boot maker in his home town. His fellow tourist and club mate 'Dicky' Eathorne, a full-back, had also spent some years in South Africa. Over the next 11 weeks Eathorne, a veteran, would find the time to make another four appearances – three away and one at home – for the Tigers.

Over Easter the Tigers scheduled three matches – at Llanelli on 18 April, Cardiff on the 20th (two days after the match against the Barbarians) and at Bristol the following day. This time the party had a significant north-eastern element. It included four Hartlepool Rovers' members who had been part of the Durham team that had been defeated by Cornwall in the County Championship Final on 28 March – Stan

Brittain, Dan Ellwood, Tom Hogarth and Joseph 'Chut' Thompson. Also, there was a place in the party for Alf Kewney, the captain of Rockliff.

What was the intention of issuing invites on such an unprecedented scale? The guests did not benefit the club's supporters because they would hardly ever appear in front of them. Did they just assist in delivering an 'attractive' team that would be worth the host club offering the Tigers a higher guarantee? Was there perhaps an element of the Tigers trying to get the same guarantees as the Barbarians? Could there have been an intention to recruit some of the guests?

Although Davey and Dyke made only those two appearances for Leicester both appear to have been on the lookout for a new club. Both players later assisted Coventry – Davey made occasional appearances and Eathorne one or two, the following season. Stan Brittain also appears to have been unsettled and soon turned professional with Hull. Whatever the reason, it was a display of Leicester largesse that could not be ignored. It threw down a challenge to the Tigers' midland enemies, as Crumbie must have realised.

Following the recall from the Anglo-Welsh tour of Fred Jackson, the Tigers were still at the forefront of the professionalism question in rugby union, as outlined in the book.

Having lost three forwards and with the club's conduct once more in question it might have been expected that Crumbie would have kept a low profile. He didn't. As soon as the new season opened Crumbie invited Tom Hogarth to turn out for Leicester. Although Hartlepool Rovers' officials had granted Hogarth's handful of previous requests, generally to take part in the Tigers' Easter tour, (they were a regular host of the Tigers on New Year tours), they must have been surprised when he accompanied their party to Leicester on Saturday 12 September 1908 with the intention of playing for the home team.

After playing against his own club Hogarth received further invitations from the Tigers and that led Hartlepool Rovers to consider complaining. Hogarth obviously enjoyed the invitations for not long after the start of the season he resigned from Rovers (a club he had joined around the turn of the century) and joined Durham City. He was listed as a Durham City representative when he appeared for Durham against Australia on 31 October 1908. The implication was that he could clearly expect no interference over his personal choices from Durham City. That switch left unanswered the question – how could a shipyard blacksmith like Hogarth afford to appear for Leicester on a regular basis? Hogarth's brother appeared for the Tigers on the New Year 1909 tour.

It was less of a question for a marine engineer like Kewney, who made only occasional appearances for the Tigers. Kewney continued to be one of the mainstays of the Northumberland pack and his occasional visits to Leicester did not harm his international career.

Threat of a new split

Around the start of October 1908 the *Leicester Daily Mercury* began to carry reports that a number of senior clubs were unhappy with the RFU and its narrow view of amateurism. While those senior clubs did not want to allow professionalism because of the way the NU had suffered as a result, they did want to operate under a more liberal version of the RFU laws. Support was expected from south Wales, the west of England and the English midlands.

By November the *Leicester Daily Mercury* was able to furnish more details of the proposed body. It was planned to establish a senior league of 10 clubs. Nine members it stated were known – Bristol, Devonport Albion, Gloucester, Leicester and Plymouth from England and Cardiff, Llanelli, Newport and Swansea from Wales. The tenth place still remained vacant. The paper went on to state that meetings of clubs and counties were expected and if Leicester was expelled then the new body was certain to be formed. It did not state what would happen if Leicester managed to retain its membership of the RFU.

The Bristol centenary history records that the committee of the Bristol club was addressed on this issue by Gloucestershire president – E.S. Bostock-Smith. The speaker told the committee that the proposal was favoured by the Welsh and the Bristol committee gave the scheme its "hearty support". The members were listed as Bristol, Devonport Albion, Gloucester and Plymouth from England and Cardiff, Llanelli, Neath, Newport, Pontypool and Swansea from Wales. Discussions continued at several more committee meetings, but nothing was established.

One skeleton having been discovered it was only to be expected that a resolution would be placed before the RFU Committee at its meeting on Monday 5 October 1908 demanding that more be sought. With no room for manoeuvre the RFU Committee decided to launch another investigation into the affairs of Leicester. The RFU committee also branded another four Leicester players professional – Fred Hardyman, J. Jackson, 'Sid' Matthews and Tom Smith. Why it was felt necessary to include the first two, when they had joined Broughton Rangers over one year previously, was never explained.

As for Smith, he was still at sea returning home from Australasia with

152

the Anglo-Welsh touring party, when his suspension was announced. When the ship docked at Queenstown (Cobh) Smith was approached by NU agents and again when he disembarked at Liverpool. Smith later signed for Broughton Rangers.

Matthews' offence had been committed in 1897, when as a member of Nuneaton he had signed a NU form with Hull FC. Although he had received £1 out of pocket expenses, he had never played for Hull. Although this had not been a professionalism offence at the time, according to the rules approved on 27 May 1897, it did not stop the RFU committee 'professionalizing' him by a majority of one vote. While Matthews was deemed guilty the Tigers were technically in the clear as the offence was committed before he joined the club. During his 10 years with the Tigers, Mathews, a hard working forward, had twice served as captain of Leicester, from 1904 to 1906 and from 1907 to 1908, represented the Midland Counties on many occasions and had appeared in an England trial in 1902 without ever getting a 'cap'.

The Anglo-Welsh tourists landed at Liverpool on Saturday 10 October. John Jackett immediately travelled to Leicester and turned out for the Tigers against Bristol that same afternoon. Whatever his personal feelings were regarding the treatment of Jackson and the threat of further investigations Jackett did not let them affect his enthusiasm for the game. Just over two weeks later, on Monday 26 October, Jackett was in the Cornwall team that met the touring Wallabies in the Olympic Final at White City. Richard Jackett was also in the team. Another Cornish tourist, 'Maffer' Davey, turned out that day and was interestingly listed in the programme as being a member of the Coventry club.

At the start of November Crumbie forwarded the club's books to the RFU for auditing. A letter from Crumbie to the RFU was also published in the local press. In the letter Crumbie asked for the cases of Smith and Matthews to be re-opened so that the previous decisions might be quashed. As far as Crumbie was concerned Matthews had committed no offence under the laws which applied before 11 March 1901 and Smith's signature on a NU form had been obtained by gross misrepresentation and unlawful methods. There was no request from the club concerning Fred Jackson. Crumbie was said to have pledged his support for a press instigated plea for Matthews' reinstatement.

The Barbarians

Once it was known that Fettes-Lorettonian, a regular visitor, was going to withdraw from the 1908 Christmas Festival (only Birkenhead Park and

Penarth appeared), Leicester's officials had worked hard to find a replacement for the following year. Ignoring the club's critics, Crumbie audaciously decided to approach the Barbarians.

A key figure in this approach appears to have been Lieutenant Walter Wilson, who had been posted to the 1st Battalion of the Leicestershire Regiment when it returned from India in the summer of 1907. A product of Tonbridge School, Wilson had been capped by England while playing for Richmond earlier in 1907. He was soon invited to play for the Barbarians and took part in the Christmas 1908 tour of south Wales.

According to Nigel Starmer-Smith's history, the Barbarians agreed to the match in 1909 14 days before the committee of inquiry met at Leicester. There were no apparent problems with the date, rail connections or the match guarantee so the Barbarians management agreed and the Tigers became the third opponents – after Cardiff and Newport – on the Barbarians' next Christmas tour. The agreement of the Barbarians was a major gesture of support for the Tigers.

Lieutenant Wilson accepted an invite from Crumbie to play for Leicester, and made his debut in April 1909, to become a rare breed – both a Tiger and a Barbarian. Shortly afterwards Wilson was elected to the Barbarians' committee.

In a further demonstration of the open mindedness about the club at the highest level of the RFU, Sid Penny, one of the game's earliest specialist hookers, was called up for his only England appearance against Australia on Saturday 9 January 1909 at the age of 33.

On the following Monday the RFU committee met to decide what to do about Leicester. The RFU president, C. Arnold Crane, as someone who was personally resentful and suspicious of Leicester's success and as a representative of the Midland Counties Union, demanded Leicester's expulsion. Crane's proposal did not gain a majority on the committee. Instead it was agreed to mount a new inquiry and a three-man sub-committee was appointed by the RFU. Unable to accept the outcome, Crane, dismissing the appeal of colleagues to stay until the end of his second term, resigned the following day.

The three men appointed – T.C. Pring of Devon, the senior vice-president and the man who would replace Crane, A. Hartley (Yorkshire) and F.H. Fox (Somerset) – held meetings in Leicester at the end of that same week, on 14 and 15 January 1909. Various club officials including Crumbie were interviewed as were the most contentious of the players – Tom Hogarth (14 appearances since the start of the season), John Jackett (12 appearances since returning from Australasia), and Alf

154

Kewney (seven appearances). All their answers were considered to be satisfactory by the committee.

There was the real possibility of a major embarrassment for the RFU because Welford Road was booked to host England versus France, on Saturday 30 January, in a non-championship international. On the morning of the match the sub-committee's findings were published; its report was presented to the General Committee of the RFU, who were meeting at the Grand Hotel. On both the charges against Leicester FC, firstly that they had played F.S. Jackson, J.W. Matthews and T. Smith while knowing of their past connections with the NU, and secondly that they had recruited those three in contravention of the professional laws, the Committee of Inquiry, on the basis of evidence heard, found the club not guilty. In a statement to the General Committee the inquiry team stated clearly its views: "Your committee is strongly of the opinion that the allegations against the Leicester club are largely due to the fact that the club, having a strong team with a good match list, attracts players who are unable to get such good football in other localities, but that, however undesirable this maybe, the players have not benefited pecuniarily thereby."

With that potentially embarrassing situation dealt with the committee members were able to take their place in the stand to watch an England XV, containing three Tigers – John Jackett, Alf Kewney and the Uppingham School and Oxford University product, Frank Tarr – gain a convincing victory, 22–0.

Legend has it that after Leicester was formally cleared of all charges Crumbie suggested that the investigators should turn their attentions to the Coventry club. Whether that was true or not something spurred the announcement, in July, of an investigation into the affairs of Coventry.

At the RFU AGM in May 1909, a resolution was passed that all clubs having a gross income of £100 must submit a properly audited balance sheet through the county committee for the attention of the secretary of the RFU. In the case of a club with a gross income of £300 or more, such as Leicester, the balance sheet must have been audited by a chartered accountant.

By then the Tigers had agreed to re-enter the Midland Counties Cup after an absence of three years, but only on the understanding that they were seeded to the quarter-finals. Although still operating as an invitation side, the Tigers had a far less cosmopolitan air about them on their return to the Cup, only three of their team in the April 1909 Final – John Jackett, A.J. Hobbs and Tom Hogarth – were not locals. Among the locals was Sid Penny, who appeared in the final again the following year to crown a truly amazing career which had seen him play in all 10 of Leicester's Cup victories between 1898 and 1910. The club's second run Midlands Counties Cup run is shown below:

3 April 1909	Leicester 8 Coventry 3	Nottingham
2 April 1910	Leicester 8 Coventry 6	Nuneaton
1911	Lost to Coventry in Round Four.	
30 March 1912	Leicester 16 Coventry 0	Rugby
5 April 1913	Leicester 39 Belgrave Premier Works 8 Leicester	
1914	Lost to Coventry in the semi-final.	

Subsequently Coventry was disqualified from the competition for fielding two ineligible players. The competition was declared null and void.

Those declared professional had no choice, but to take their leave of the rugby union game. Fred Jackson chose to marry and settle in New Zealand. Tom Smith never showed much interest in his agreement with Broughton Rangers. He did however turn out for Coventry NUFC in their launch match against Rochdale Hornets on 15 January 1910. Smith did not pursue a career with them, and settled down instead to life as a publican first in Rearsby, his birthplace, and later at Spilsby.

There is a reminder of one of the expelled players' distress included in the Leicestershire Union's Centenary history. Rather than receiving plaudits at the end of his long service Matthews was banished to his cobblers shop in his home village of Oadby. His future involvement was restricted to watching Oadby's matches and attending their functions. Matthews wrote the following in a letter some months later: "I am glad there is someone who knows I have played football, some people hardly know that I have ever played football since I have been suspended. I am sorry such a thing happened but it was no secret to the Leicester Committee that I had signed a Northern Union form. Second thought, it would have been the last thing I should have thought of playing with a professional football team. Hope in time I shall be reinstated and give help to junior football in Leicester." Sadly his hopes of reinstatement were never realised.

John Jackett, Jackson's team mate for the Tigers, Cornwall, England and the Anglo-Welsh, saw his 13 cap England career end in March 1909. He carried on playing for the Tigers, and shared full-back duties with Dan Ellwood. After playing his last game for Leicester on 2 December 1911, Jackett belatedly turned professional, aged nearly 30, with Dewsbury. He enjoyed a great first season that culminated in a Challenge Cup Final victory over Oldham. Jackett's playing career was later ended by a broken jaw, sustained in a match against Coventry.

156

Two of those closely questioned by the inquisitors were able to choose when to take their leave. Although he made the last of his 32 appearances for Durham in 1908–09, Tom Hogarth continued to play regularly for the Tigers up to 1912 when he was in his mid-thirties. After that his appearances declined, and he made his one 111th and last appearance for the Tigers on 14 April 1914. Alf Kewney, five years Hogarth's junior, made his 27th and last appearance for the Tigers on 2 January 1913 – just prior to collecting his 16th and last England cap against South Africa on 4 January.

The Northern Union in the midlands

As honorary secretary, Crumbie received an inquiry from the NU about staging a test match against the touring professional New Zealand 'All Golds' at Welford Road in February 1908. It was possible – Welford Road was not required on Saturday 15 February when the Tigers had a match at Swansea, but Leicester's refusal was read to the members of the NU committee at their meeting on 12 November 1907. The meeting also heard that an approach to Leicester Fosse about the possibility of using Filbert Street – Saturday 22 February was available when City had an away match against Derby County – had also been refused. Rejection by both clubs meant there was no way the NU could stage a tour match in Leicester.

In the summer of 1909 the professionalism issue resurfaced in the Midlands. The outcome of the RFU's investigation into the Coventry club was that an independent NU club emerged and began operating in the city. Among those suspended by the RFU for acts of professionalism were 'Dicky' Eathorne and 'Maffer' Davey.

This had some major political repercussions for Leicester. When Coventry RUFC was suspended in October 1909 for alleged professionalism, Manchester FC wrote to the RFU warning of the harm that would be caused to the game if the NU was able to gain a foothold in the Midlands as a result of any proposed disciplinary action. That letter was if anything just a reinforcement for an approach to professionalism that had already been adopted by the RFU leadership – that it must not be allowed to spread beyond the northern region at any cost. There would be no more investigations into the Tigers' affairs as the RFU concentrated on suppressing any NU threat.

As if to allay Leicester fears that the club might be still under suspicion, a very public act of support was forthcoming when Stratford-upon-Avon provided the opposition on the opening day of the new season. On that day, Saturday 4 September 1909, the new clubhouse, built behind the goals at the Aylestone Road end of the ground, at a cost of £1,150, was officially opened by the former honorary secretary and president of the RFU, G. Rowland Hill. During the opening ceremony Hill spelt out the reason for his attendance – he wanted to show that he considered Leicester conducted its affairs by the rules of the RFU.

While sorting out details of the Barbarians' visit it was business as usual at Welford Road. The new season was only a few weeks old before the Hartlepool Rovers committee, upset at the calls on the services of their County full-back, Dan Ellwood, wrote to Leicester, and considered an approach to the RFU. They asked Leicester to reduce the number of invitations to their leading players as it was affecting gates at the Friarage. Ellwood's decision to follow Hogarth's path and join Durham City in November 1909 rendered Rovers' protests redundant. Rovers also regularly lost players to the NU at this time.

Nearer to home the Tigers issued an invitation to the captain of Rugby FC, W.J. 'Jimmy' Allen, to turn out for them. Allen accepted the Tigers' offer and joined them on a trip to Newport on 20 November 1909. He played in the first and third matches of Leicester's Christmas festival – against Cinderford and Penarth – and was included in the Tigers team, alongside Ellwood, Hogarth and Jackett, to meet the Barbarians when they arrived at Welford Road on Wednesday 29 December 1909. A crowd of more than 10,000 saw the Barbarians, captained by Walter Wilson, held to a 9–9 draw. The Tigers' could not have received a better expression of establishment support than to have the Barbarians pay the club a visit so soon after a major professional inquiry. Having found the fixture mutually beneficial the two invitation clubs agreed to make it a regular Christmas event.

Allen accompanied the Tigers on their northern tour to play Hartlepool Rovers and Headingley over New Year 1910. By the time the party returned to Leicester, Allen had decided to switch clubs. Even though it was mid-season Allen resigned the captaincy and his membership of Rugby FC and threw in his lot with the Tigers.

The visit of Northampton to Welford Road on Saturday 10th December 1910 produced an extremely vigorous match. A number of players were injured and Crumbie made strong complaints immediately afterwards about the questionable tactics employed by certain of the visitors. On the following Tuesday morning a letter from Crumbie arrived at Northampton informing the club that his committee had decided, "in the interests of the game", to cancel next season's fixtures unless the Saints issued an apology and punished three of their players. Northampton denied all the accusations. If no action was to be taken then Crumbie demanded that three players – Williamson, Hives and Cook – should be banned from facing Leicester again. This demand was also dismissed and the dispute settled diplomatically. The presence of R. Hives in the Northampton ranks, he had left Leicester in 1908 after three seasons, always rankled with Crumbie.

After 1910 the number of guests included in the Tigers' team dropped, their places being occupied by a growing number of locals. Strategically the use of guests appeared to have done its job. One of the longest serving invitees was Dan Ellwood, but just when he probably thought that he had made the Tigers' full-back position his own, he suffered a broken collarbone, sustained in his 33rd county appearance for Durham against Northumberland on 20 January 1912. Although Ellwood made a handful of appearances for the Tigers in 1912–13 and 1913–14, that injury effectively ended his playing career.

Being acknowledged as Midlands' champions helped further improve the fixture list. Harlequins were added in March 1909 and the following year Leicester travelled to meet them at their new home – and beat them 3-0 – the National Rugby Stadium at Twickenham. Blackheath travelled to Welford Road on 4 February 1911. That match, which ended in 9-9 draw, marked the start of an annual fixture exchange. To make spaces those old adversaries, Hartlepool Rovers, were dropped from the Tigers' fixture list in 1911–12. Oxford University returned to the fixture list in 1912–13, having withdrawn from playing the club in 1908. As the second decade of the 20th century got underway the Tigers had an impressive fixture list that featured the leading clubs in England, Scotland and Wales.

Tom Crumbie was indefatigable, carrying on regardless, striving to maintain the freedoms necessary to allow a gate-taking senior club to function successfully. In practice it required the Welsh halfway house model – halfway between amateurism and professionalism – to be allowed to work in English Rugby Union. Crumbie remained centrally involved in the district – accepting the Presidency of the Leicester Schools Football League (Rugby Union) in 1912.

Although there was no club fixture, Welford Road hosted a crowd of 16,000, on Saturday 9 November, to watch the second Springboks defeat a Midland Counties XV, containing 11 Tigers, 25–3. Although the playing personnel were changing the club still relied on a strong, powerful pack as the basis for its style of play. The standing of the Tigers as the best team in the Midlands and generally the provinces remained unchallenged.

A visit to the Rectory Field, Blackheath on the Saturday before Christmas 1912 brought a 27–14 victory. During the season the Tigers managed to beat Newport 6–0, one of only two clubs to manage that, and draw with both Cardiff 3–3 and the Welsh champions Swansea 0–0 at Welford Road. Over Christmas the Tigers, with four England internationals in the team – Lawrie, Tarr, Taylor and Ward, secured a narrow victory, 15–11, over a strong Barbarian XV. As expected the Tigers beat Belgrave Premier Works in the Cup Final to regain the title of Midlands champions. At the end of the season the Tigers' record earned the club the reputation of being England's champion club. The Tigers' last match of the season, against a London XV, was played as a benefit for Leicestershire County Cricket Club. By 1913 the Tigers' Football League Second Division neighbours, Leicester Fosse, had huge accumulated debts.

Individual Tigers continued to win international caps. Wyggeston School old boy, Percy Lawrie, should have earned more than his two caps, both against Scotland, in March 1910 and March 1911. Lawrie, the Tigers' captain, was chosen to play against Wales in January 1911, but as far as the England selection committee was concerned, he was a wet weather wing, and as the day of the match was fine, he was replaced at the last minute. He was prevented from playing against Ireland in February 1911 by a broken wrist.

Belgrave product, George Ward, won his first England cap as a specialist hooker at Cardiff in January 1913. After appearing against France, Ward decided that international rugby did not appeal to him and declined selection for the match against Ireland in February. Fortunately he was persuaded otherwise and was recalled to the England side for the Calcutta Cup match in March.

After an interval of four years, Frank Tarr was recalled and won a fourth England cap in the centres against Scotland on 15 March 1913.

When the Tigers travelled to Gloucester on the first Saturday of January 1914 they did so without seven regular first teamers – all of whom were appearing in the England versus the Rest trial at Twickenham. George Ward and the Tigers' half-back pairing, Fred 'Tim' Taylor and George 'Pedlar' Wood, were subsequently chosen to play for England in the win over Wales on 17 January 1914. Taylor, the stand-off, and Wood, the scrum-half, were products of the local elementary schools, Medway Street and Melbourne Road respectively, and gave long service to the Tigers. However, this was their only appearance for England. Ward went on to collect another two caps before withdrawing from the team that travelled to Paris to play France in April.

One of the young forwards becoming prominent was Frank 'Sos' Taylor, Fred's brother, who had appeared in the first Schools International in 1904 while at Medway Street School before making his debut for the Tigers on 28 January 1911. Due to unforeseen circumstances he would have to wait until 1920 to win the first of his two England caps.

Crumbie had some major plans in the pipeline as the close season of 1914 approached. Undaunted by the opening of Twickenham, the club had proceeded to reconstruct the members' stand, at a cost of £13,000, and the official opening was expected in the autumn of 1914. As a result, Welford Road was by then, without doubt, the best provincial rugby union ground in England.

The break-up of the Midland Counties Union

Rumblings of discontent over the structure of the Midland Counties Union had begun to translate into calls for action by Christmas 1913. On 26 January 1914, junior clubs in Leicestershire requested a meeting with the Tigers' committee to discuss forming a Leicestershire County Union independent of the Midland Counties Union.

Against this background the Midland Counties defeated Cornwall in front of 6,000 spectators at Welford Road on 18 February to progress to the County Championship final. On 28 March 1914 Welford Road hosted the final, where a Midland Counties XV, containing 10 Tigers, two of them replacements for club colleagues, beat Durham to become champions for the first and only time.

After months of argument in the press, the case for the break-up of the regional body came to the Midland Counties Union AGM. It was a stormy meeting that saw the Union's longstanding president, E.B. Holmes of Moseley, deposed. Crumbie was incensed by the way Holmes was treated and said, at a meeting of Leicestershire clubs on Friday 26 June 1914, that the Tigers could no longer remain members. He then proposed, and the meeting agreed that the only course of action, subject to RFU approval, was to reconstruct the Leicestershire Rugby Union as an independent, nationally recognised body.

At last the Tigers and Leicestershire were free of the Midland Counties Union. This was a radical departure that would force the Tigers out of the Midland Counties Cup and into responsibility, as by far the strongest club, for the team that would be entered into the County Championship.

The First World War

Much to the surprise of many, war was declared just as the first practice matches were being organised for the new season. Frank Tarr, a member of the Territorials, reported for duty on 4 August and was sent to join the 4th Leicestershire Regiment.

Nine days later, on 13 August 1914, the RFU issued a circular that advised all players to join the armed forces. Saddled with major debts Leicester initially intended to carry on and the traditional season opener, against an Alliance XV, went ahead as normal on 2 September, but problems with finding opponents caused the Committee to reconsider and closedown for the duration. Very soon Welford Road would be the headquarters for two artillery units and a pioneer corps.

The outbreak of war brought to a close a turbulent but increasingly prosperous 20 years for the Leicester club. That it had survived as a member of the RFU was in some ways remarkable. What were the reasons for its survival?

Was NRL membership considered to be so unattractive or uneconomic in terms of travel and support? Were the Tigers inherently loyal to the RFU? Was a switch considered too dangerous in terms of breaking up local unity and allowing professional association football to expand? Was the price of failure imposed by the RFU, if a switch was made, just too high for the Tigers to consider?

By surviving the club had shown that a major gate-taking club could successfully function within the RFU, albeit with a very high profile fixture list. Leagues and overt professionalism in Leicester's case had not proved necessary.

Bibliography

New Zealand newspapers
Ashburton Guardian
Bay of Plenty Times
Canterbury Times
The Colonist
Evening Post (Wellington)
Gray River Argos
Hawera and Normandy Star
Nelson Evening News
New Zealand Tablet
New Zealand Truth
Observer
Otago Witness
Poverty Bay Herald
he Bystander
The Star
Taranaki Herald
Wanganui Herald

Australian newspapers
The Referee
Sydney Morning Herald
Sydney Daily Telegraph
The Sun

British newspapers
Athletic News
Camborne Times
Cambrian
Daily Chronicle
Leicester Mercury
Manchester Guardian
The Salford Journal
The Salford Reporter
South Wales Evening Post
South Wales Times
The Standard
The Times

The Western Mail
West Briton
The York Herald

Books and magazines
The British Tourists in Maoriland – True History of the tour by R.A. Barr
Rugby's Great Split by Tony Collins
The Best in the Northern Union by Tom Mather
All Blacks v Lions by Ron Palenski
Te Araroa an East Coast community – A history by Bob McConnell
The Original All Blacks by Christopher Tobin
Code 13 magazine
Cardiff Evening Express

Bibliography for Appendix 2

Barron, Brian	*Oh When the Saints* (Northampton, 1993)
Bowker, Barry	*North Midlands Rugby* (Birmingham, 1970)
Bromley, Martin (Bill)	*One Hundred Years of Rugby in Oadby* (Oadby, 1988)
Farmer, Stuart & Hands, David	*The Tigers Tale* (Leicester, 1993)
Hands, David	*Leicester F.C. 1880 – 1980* (Leicester, 1980)
Haynes, John	*From All Blacks to All Golds* (Christchurch, 1996)
Keen, Dennis	*The Rugby Lions* (Rugby, 1991)
Hopkins, S.I. 'Van'	*Leicestershire Rugby Union 1887 – 1987* (Leicester, 1986)
Kemp, Robert M.L.	*Stoneygate F.C. 1888 – 1988* (Leicester, 1988)
Leicestershire Schools R.F.U.	*Centenary 1894 – 1994* (Leicester, 1994)
Lister, Fred	*Hartlepool Rovers F.C. 1879 – 1979* (Hartlepool, 1979)
Maule, Raymond	*The Complete Who's Who of England Rugby Union Internationals* (Derby, 1992)
Redruth R.F.C.	*Centenary 1875 – 1975* (Redruth, 1975)
Starmer-Smith, Nigel	*The Barbarians* (London, 1977)
Thompson, Brian	*Leicester Tigers* (Leicester, 1947)

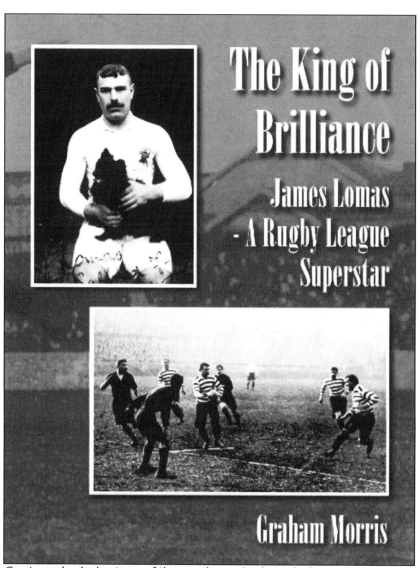

Great new book about one of the sport's genuine legends. James Lomas played for Bramley, Salford, Oldham and York, and won representative honours for Lancashire, Cumberland, England and Great Britain. He captained the first Lions tourists in 1910. This is the first biography of him.
Published in October 2011 at £16.95 (hardback).
Signed copies available direct from London League Publications Ltd,
PO Box 65784, London NW2 9NS (cheques payable to London League Publications Ltd); credit card orders via our website: www.llpshop.co.uk

Best in the Northern Union

The pioneering 1910
Rugby League Lions tour
of Australia and New Zealand

Tom Mather

Fascinating account of the first Great Britain Lions tour of Australia and New Zealand. Published in 2010 at £12.95, special offer £12.00 direct from London League Publications Ltd. Credit card orders via www.llpshop.co.uk , orders by cheque to LLP, PO Box 65784, London NW2 9NS

Jack Fish
A Rugby League Superstar

By Gary Slater

Jack Fish was one of the sport's great players from the Northern Union period.

He played for Warrington, Lancashire and England. He played in four Challenge Cup Finals, and scored both tries when Warrington beat Hull KR 6–0 in 1905. He captained the team in 1907 when they beat Oldham 17–3 in the Final.
He scored a phenomenal 214 tries and kicked 263 goals for the Wire. He is still the only player to score 200 tries and kick 200 goals for Warrington.

This book is the first biography of Jack Fish. It will be published in April 2011, at £11.95. Order from London League Publications Ltd direct for just £11.00. . Credit card orders via www.llpshop.co.uk order by cheque to LLP, PO Box 65784, London NW2 9NS

Ces Mountford was a great player for West Coast in New Zealand, and then for Wigan. He then coached Warrington in the 1950s before returning to New Zealand where he became the New Zealand national coach and did great work developing coaching and rugby league in the country.

George Nepia was one of the New Zealand's greatest rugby players. He played rugby union for the All Blacks, and as a 19-year-old was their full-back on their 1924-35 unbeaten tour of Great Britain and France.
In 1935 he switched to rugby league and joined Streatham & Mitcham RLFC in London, and then played for Halifax before returning to New Zealand where he became a dual international by playing for the Kiwis. He was subsequently reinstated into rugby union after the Second World War.